'Ros Clarke's *Human* is a fresh, inspiring deep dive into what it m navel-gazing or indulgence, she of uniquely comes from the God wh_ _____ us. She helps us understand what we once were, what we should be and what in Christ we will be again. On top of all that, Ros manages to pack into a highly readable and accessible book a serious engagement with important controversies in the wider culture that affect us all. This is a really helpful book that I hope is read far and wide.'
Revd Dr Mark Meynell, Director (Europe & Caribbean), Langham Preaching, and author of *A Wilderness of Mirrors*, *When Darkness Seems My Closest Friend* and *What Makes Us Human?*

'*Human* is super readable; fresh and relevant in content, clear in style – exactly what we have come to expect from Ros Clarke! There are honest insights on work, the body and soul, sexuality and many other topics. All the while, Clarke continues to unpack who we are, made in the image of God. The book doesn't stop there, however, but crescendos in the New Man, Christ Jesus, securing a new redeemed humanity for himself. This book is a great, gospel-centred and countercultural antidote to these mad days of self-made humanity.
Natalie Brand, Bible teacher and author of *Priscilla, Where Are You? A Call to Joyful Theology*

'In an age confused about what it means to be human, we desperately need books like this! Clear and accessible, rich and deep, biblically faithful and beautifully written, *Human* demonstrates the relevance and power of the Bible to show us who we really are and who we're meant to be.'
Matthew Mason, Assistant Director, Pastors' Academy, and Director, Crosslands Cultivate.

HUMAN

HUMAN

Made and remade in the image of God

Ros Clarke

INTER-VARSITY PRESS
36 Causton Street, London SW1P 4ST, England
Email: ivp@ivpbooks.com
Website: www.ivpbooks.com

First published 2023

British Library Cataloguing-in-Publication Data

A catalogue record for this book is available from the British Library.

ISBN: 978–1–78974–483–5
eBook ISBN: 978–1–78974–484–2

Set in Minion Pro 11.75/15.5pt
Typeset in Great Britain by CRB Associates, Potterhanworth, Lincolnshire
Printed and bound in Great Britain by Ashford Colour Press Ltd

Produced on paper from sustainable sources

Inter-Varsity Press publishes Christian books that are true to the Bible and that communicate the gospel, develop discipleship and strengthen the church for its mission in the world.

IVP originated within the Inter-Varsity Fellowship, now the Universities and Colleges Christian Fellowship, a student movement connecting Christian Unions in universities and colleges throughout Great Britain, and a member movement of the International Fellowship of Evangelical Students. Website: www.uccf.org.uk. That historic association is maintained, and all senior IVP staff and committee members subscribe to the UCCF Basis of Faith.

Contents

Acknowledgements

Many thanks to Joshua Wells of IVP and Elizabeth McQuoid of Keswick Ministries for their guidance and help in producing this book. Thanks are also due to Matthew Mason, not only for reading an early draft and giving invaluable feedback, but also for leading a study day on transgender that shaped my thinking on some of the most complex issues in the book. I am constantly grateful for my employers at Church Society for their encouragement in all the different aspects of my work, and especially for my boss, Lee Gatiss.

Acknowledgements

Introduction

Let me introduce myself at the beginning of this book. I'm Ros, but on my birth certificate it says 'Rosalind Sarah Clarke'. I'm 49 years old, white British, and I live in Stafford, in central England. That's probably enough information to identify me, though there are other details I could give but prefer not to make so public!

That kind of identification doesn't tell you very much about me. It doesn't tell you who I am as a person. So let me try again.

I'm Ros. I am the Associate Director of Church Society and Course Leader for the Priscilla Programme. At various times in my life, I've been a chef, a maths teacher, an administrator and in full-time Christian ministry. I design knitting and cross-stitch patterns as a sideline. I love art and making, and I am very lazy at housework.

If you were to read my full CV, you'd get a whole lot more detail about what I do and what I have done in my life. That tells you a bit about my story and the kind of things I'm good at, as well as what I enjoy. But I am more than the things I do.

Let's try a different approach. I'm Ros, and I'm Liz and Ivor's daughter. My grandparents were Betty and Kenneth, Nancy and Ivor. I'm Richard's sister and Kate's sister-in-law. I'm Cameron and Sophie's aunt, and cousin to a lot of people. I'm Thomas and Elliot's godmother, and I'm friends with lots of people, including Dawn (who will be delighted to get a mention in the book). I'm part of the family at Castle Church.

That's how a lot of people in the Bible are identified: as part of a family network. We all have that network of friends, family, colleagues and church. Our relationships are a vital part of who we are and where we fit in the world. But that would be an unusual way to identify ourselves in the contemporary world, and again it feels as though it misses out quite a lot of what is important about who we are.

In this book we are going to see what the Bible's answer is to the question of who we are as human beings. Here's how I might describe myself using the criteria we'll find there.

I'm Ros. I'm made by God and made in his image. I'm female and I'm single. I'm created for useful work and to be part of a community. I'm a sinner and I am mortal: I am going to die. But I have been redeemed by Christ and given new life by his Spirit. I have been adopted into God's family as his beloved child. I am part of the new humanity that Christ is building across every tribe and nation, every language and every ethnicity. I am confidently looking forward to resurrection life in the new creation, with God, for ever.

What does that tell you about me? Everything that is important about being human.

Questions of human identity have become pivotal in society over the past ten or fifteen years. Simple questions that were so obvious most of us never bothered to ask them are now touchstones of political correctness and self-determination: What is a woman? What is a human being? Who decides who or what I am? A feature-length documentary released in 2022 was dedicated to the first of those questions.[1] Politicians who

---

1 Matt Walsh, 'What Is a Woman?', Daily Wire, 2022: <https://www.dailywire.com/videos/what-is-a-woman> (accessed 10 February 2023).

are asked about these issues stumble to find answers, and when they do, they almost always have to be retracted the next day. How has it become so hard to know who we are?

Are human beings simply a highly developed species of ape? Is a woman a person who feels like a woman, no matter what their physical body is like? Can I self-identify my gender or my race, or are those imposed on me by others? Is my body part of me, or just a sophisticated carrier bag for the 'real' me?

Reality seems to be rapidly spiralling away from us. It is no surprise that the further society moves away from its Christian heritage and influence, the weaker its grasp becomes on all kinds of other questions. If we have no agreed starting point for ethics, anthropology or sociology, we should expect to find ourselves confused about what is right, how to be human and how to live in community.

If we want to know what it means to be human, self-examination may seem like a good idea, but it turns out to be of limited use. First, because we can only know ourselves, not other people, by this route. If I look only at myself, I can't tell what is unique to me because of my particular personality and circumstances, and what is common to all humanity. Is it fundamental to being human that you love hot pink and cross stitch? Probably not, but those things matter to me!

Second, simply examining ourselves is of limited use because we are all sinners. And, as we'll see, that affects our ability to understand anything well. Sin affects our thinking as much as our emotions and desires. So our conclusions about humanity based on our own investigation are likely to be flawed.

Third, we can never be impartial observers of ourselves. We have a vested interest in who and what we are. Our observations are always going to be biased. We should expect to have huge blind spots as we examine our own character and self.

Fourth, we can't see the whole picture. We exist in the present moment, and although we have some memory of the past, we certainly don't know our whole lives. Even less do we know about where we have come from: our ancestors and our creation. Nor can we see where we are heading, in this life and beyond. Our experience of our own humanity is limited.

If we truly want to understand what it means to be human, we have to look beyond humanity. We need God to explain it to us. God can tell us who we were made to be and why. He can explain what is distinctive about humanity and what our purpose is in creation. God knows how our humanity has been distorted by sin and how it is being restored in Christ. God sees the whole picture. His judgement is not limited, and it is not distorted by sin.

In this book, then, we will go back to the beginning, to see what God tells us about human beings in creation. We will trace those themes throughout the Bible, to see how Christ himself shows us most fully what it means to be human. We'll consider how our humanity has been spoiled by sin and the effects of living in a fallen world. Finally, we'll think about how our humanity is being restored now in Christ, by his Spirit, and what we are looking forward to in the final resurrection when we will be truly, fully human as God intended.

I hope you will learn more about yourself as you read this book and especially as you consider the Bible passages and think about the questions in the study guide. But I hope for more than that. I hope you will learn more about all humanity, this vast and wonderfully glorious race to which we all belong and which will one day be united together in worship of the living God. I hope that you will learn to celebrate your humanness, in all its purpose and all its limitations, and to have confidence in who you are, as God made you to be.

1

Being human means being created

In the beginning, God created the heavens and the earth. He made the light and the dark, the night and the day. He made the sea and the land, and he filled both with every kind of plant and animal, fish and bird, insect and reptile. And then, in his glorious final flourish of creation, he made human beings. Those first human beings were made in unique ways to indicate that they stand at the head of the whole human race. There is no chicken-or-egg dilemma in the Bible's account of humanity.

God made the very first human beings and God makes all human beings. Every single person who has ever lived, and every single person who *will* ever live, is made by God. The rest of us are not made in quite the same way as Adam and Eve. As the psalmist puts it, he knitted us together in our mother's womb (Psalm 139:13).

This is where we must begin in our understanding of what it means to be human: we are created beings, made by God, given value by God, given a purpose by God and utterly dependent on God.

You are made by God

When God created the universe he did not begin by collecting together his materials. He was not a sculptor forming a shape out of clay, or a carpenter nailing his wood together. God created the universe out of nothing. There was nothing to start with. He generated the very atoms and molecules that he shaped into planets and stars, seas and land, plants and animals.

But when God creates human beings now he does not begin with nothing. He creates us through the joining of an egg and a sperm, which usually takes place in a woman's fallopian tube. This fertilised egg makes its way into the womb, where it multiplies cells and grows into a human body. Ultrasound scans from about nine weeks after fertilisation of that single cell already show recognisably human forms.

Human beings cannot control this process. No matter how often a couple has sex, nor how sophisticated fertility treatments become, there is no guarantee of success. There is currently no obvious scientific reason why some couples who have struggled with infertility for years suddenly conceive after they have given up hope. The reverse is also true: no contraception is 100% proof against pregnancy. We cannot say why this egg will fertilise, but not that one. We cannot say which sperm will be the one to fertilise the egg.

What we *can* say is that every single time a child is conceived it is because God has breathed life into that fertilised cell. It is because God is beginning his work of knitting a new person together.

We can have absolute confidence, therefore, that we are here because God made us. God planned and designed and created you. There are no accidents – happy or otherwise – in God's fertility clinic. You may have wonderful human parents, or terrible ones. You may have always known the security of being wanted and loved by your family, or you may have never known that. But know this: God wanted you. God wanted precisely you, with your specific DNA, and your specific date and time of birth, and your particular biological parents. God knitted you together so you would be just that tall, and have just that skin tone, and hair which curls in just that way. God made you to have your unique personality and your specific talents.

Let's look at Psalm 139 again:

For you created my inmost being;
   you knit me together in my mother's womb.
I praise you because I am fearfully and wonderfully
      made;
   your works are wonderful,
   I know that full well.
(Psalm 139:13–14)

You are made by God, and he made you wonderfully. God did not make a mistake when he made you. Praise God!

You are valued by God

Sometimes on *Antiques Roadshow* two different objects of the same kind will be brought in to be examined and valued. One might appear to be in better condition, but the other might have a more attractive design. The valuer will point out all kinds of details the owner has never noticed, and then finally comes the moment we've all been waiting for, the money moment. But the value of each object doesn't just depend on its design or condition. Its value also depends on its maker. A landscape by John Constable will be worth many thousands of times more than a similar painting by an unknown artist. A cabinet designed by Thomas Chippendale will command a far higher price than one by Mr Anon or Mrs IKEA.

It is the same with you and me. Our value cannot be calculated simply by looking at our external appearance, our beauty or our condition. Our value comes from our Maker. You are that wonderful thing: a human being made by Almighty God, Lord of heaven and earth. Therefore you are of immense, incalculable value.

This is what Psalm 8 has to say about the worth of human beings:

> You have made them a little lower than the angels
>   and crowned them with glory and honour.
> (Psalm 8:5)

God himself has crowned human beings with glory and honour. I think that is one of the most extraordinary things the Bible says. God honours us. God gives us glory. Not because we have earned it, but because human beings are the pinnacle of God's creation, made in his image. We are glorified because he is glorious. We are honoured because he is worthy of all honour.

I said at the beginning of this book that if we want to understand what it truly means to be human, we need to listen to God rather than look inside ourselves. This is one good example of that. It is very common for people to have a low view of themselves. We all know our own flaws better than anyone else. We can see all the mistakes we've made, all the weaknesses we struggle with and all the challenges we've failed. When we measure our own worth, we compare ourselves to others. And it's always easy to find someone more successful, more beautiful, richer, cleverer, happier. Especially if we're on social media.

We live in a particularly judgemental culture at the moment, where everyone's life is on public display for scrutiny and comment; where it's normal to pick apart a person's parenting skills or choice of hobby; where we all feel the need to put on a mask when we share our lives, in order to protect ourselves from attack. Of course, people struggle with low self-esteem in this sort of culture. Teenagers (both boys and girls) are especially vulnerable to this. Where once they could be protected from this endless judgement in the safety of home, now they are vulnerable any time they have a phone in their hand.

But here's the thing. Your true value doesn't depend on what the world thinks you are worth. It doesn't matter what your salary is or your social status. It doesn't matter if you have disabilities or chronic illness. It doesn't matter how well your appearance matches modern standards of beauty. It doesn't matter whether you are tall or short, fat or thin, rich or poor, clever or ordinary, successful or plodding. None of those things can add to the value you have as one of God's precious creations. None of those things can take away from that value. He has crowned you with glory and honour. You are infinitely valuable because you are made by God. You are infinitely valuable because you are *wonderfully* made by God, who does not make mistakes.

That is not to say, of course, that you are morally perfect. We are all sinners and we'll consider how that affects our humanity in a later chapter. But even our sin does not destroy our worth as people made by God.

11

You have been given a purpose by God

One of the ways in which the Bible commonly talks about human beings as God's creations is by comparing us to clay in the hands of a potter. The clay begins in one amorphous lump and it can be shaped and formed into any number of different items by a skilled potter. The same clay can be used to make beautiful works of art, practical plates and bowls, or even serve our most basic functional needs in the form of toilets. The clay does not get to choose what it will become. The potter is in control.

Isaiah uses this imagery to point out that God knew what he was doing when he made us:

> You turn things upside down,
>   as if the potter were thought to be like the clay!
> Shall what is formed say to the one who formed it,
>   'You did not make me'?
> Can the pot say to the potter,
>   'You know nothing'?
> (Isaiah 29:16)

It is intentionally ludicrous. Of course the pot can't say that! The pot knows nothing, while the potter knows precisely what the pot is intended for. Don't be like the foolishly arrogant pot! God did make you and God does know what he is doing.

Paul cites Isaiah in Romans 9, using this same image of the potter and the clay, when he is explaining God's election of some people to salvation and others to destruction:

> But who are you, a human being, to talk back to God?
> 'Shall what is formed say to the one who formed it,

"Why did you make me like this?"' Does not the potter have the right to make out of the same lump of clay some pottery for special purposes and some for common use?
(Romans 9:20–1)

Pots don't get to decide what they are for. Clay doesn't get to tell the potter what it wants to be. The potter, obviously, is the one in charge. The potter has the right to decide, and so does God. God gets to decide what he has made us for. In Paul's discussion he is talking about the final purpose of human beings in eternity, but it is also true about our purpose here on earth.

In Ephesians, Paul describes us as 'God's handiwork, created in Christ Jesus to do good works, which God prepared in advance for us to do' (Ephesians 2:10). In Jeremiah, God tells his people through the prophet that he knows the plans he has for them (Jeremiah 29:11). Proverbs tells us that, while we may make our own plans, it is God who determines our steps (Proverbs 16:9). The Bible is clear throughout that God is in control and God has plans for us. God has a purpose for each of us. He has prepared works for us to do – works that he has created us to do.

We are made by God for the purpose he has determined. He knows what he has planned for you to do, and he has created you with that purpose in mind. He has created you with the specific talents and skills, the particular networks of family and friends, the precise opportunities and challenges, for you to fulfil his purpose for your life. He has prepared works in advance for you to do, and you can be sure that he has designed and made you perfectly to be able to do them. He is, after all, the Master Potter.

Later in the book we'll think more about what purpose God has made us for, but for now we can simply hold on to the fact that our lives are not meaningless or pointless. There is a purpose for all humanity and each of us is needed to accomplish that. God has made you, specifically you, for a purpose that matters.

You are dependent on God

Think about those pots again. How does a pot decide to come into being? It doesn't, of course! A pot is wholly dependent on the potter for its existence. Now think about yourself. How did you decide to come into being? You didn't, of course. Your parents may have hoped and tried, but they needed God to bring you into being. Your parents may have longed for a child, but they could not have known they wanted you specifically. Every child is a surprise to their parents, who will spend years discovering what their offspring is like. But none of us is a surprise to God. He knew precisely what he was knitting together.

We all depended on God to bring us into existence and we all continue to depend on God for our ongoing existence every single day of our lives. This is how Jesus explained it to his disciples:

> Look at the birds of the air; they do not sow or reap or store away in barns, and yet your heavenly Father feeds them. Are you not much more valuable than they? Can any one of you by worrying add a single hour to your life?
> (Matthew 6:26–7)

If God, our heavenly Father, provides the birds of the air with everything they need, how much more will he look after us, his precious children? We need not worry, Jesus says, because we can trust God. And we should not worry, because worrying is pointless. We cannot keep ourselves alive even for an hour by worrying. God is in control and we are dependent on him for our ongoing existence.

This doesn't mean that we always need God to provide miraculously for us. God normally provides through ordinary ways for us – just as he does for the birds. That means we work to earn money for food and clothing and shelter, and we visit doctors and dentists for medical care. It means we trust in God to give us what we need in whatever ways he chooses. But even when he provides through those ordinary ways, we must remember that it is God who provides.

A good way to do this is to pray like the Puritan author of 'The All-Good', who asked:

> Grant me to feel thee in fire, and food and every
>   providence,
> and to see that thy many gifts and creatures
> are but thy hands and fingers taking hold of me.[1]

When you look around at all the good things in your life, remember that they come from God, who is taking care of you. When you depend on your central heating to keep you warm in winter, or your car to get you to work, remember that God has provided them for you. When you collect your

---

1 Arthur Bennett (ed.), *The Valley of Vision: A collection of prayers and devotions* (Edinburgh: Banner of Truth, 1975), p. 7.

prescription from the pharmacy, thank God, who has made that possible. When you have food on the table, give thanks to God, who sustains you every hour of every day of your life.

If we are dependent on God, that means we are not independent beings. We cannot simply rely on ourselves. We must admit that we cannot provide for all our needs. We cannot make all our own decisions. We do not know best.

Acknowledging that we are created, dependent beings is humbling. We don't like to think of ourselves as needy. We don't always like to admit that we need support, advice or instruction. We certainly don't like to be recipients of charity.

But we are all, whether we admit it or not, utterly dependent on God. We constantly need him for our ongoing existence. We need him to tell us what we are here for and how to live according to the manufacturer's instructions. We can't earn any of those things from him – it is all a free gift of his grace.

There is the paradox: as created human beings we find that we have infinitely precious value, but we also recognise that we are utterly dependent on God for everything. I don't know which of these truths you most need to hear right now. Perhaps you are struggling with low self-esteem and need to treasure those words that remind you how precious you are because you are God's wonderful creation. Perhaps you have a tendency to pride and self-reliance, and need to remember how everything you have comes from God and stop trusting in your own strength. Perhaps you need to learn how to hold on to both those truths.

Questions to consider

1 Read carefully through all of Psalm 139. What comfort and encouragement does the psalmist take from knowing that God is his Creator?

2 Are you tempted to value yourself too little or rate yourself too highly? What correctives do the Bible passages mentioned in this chapter give?

3 In what areas of your life do you find it hard to depend on God? How do the passages from Isaiah 29, Romans 9 and Matthew 6 help to put this in the right perspective?

4 Could you write your own version of the All-Good prayer quoted above, to use regularly to help you remember that the Lord provides everything for you?

5 Read through the Bible passages quoted in this chapter again. If there is one that particularly strikes you, try to memorise it, or make a note of it somewhere you will see it regularly, to remind you of your status as a created human being.

2

Being human means being in the image of God

At the point in creation when God turned his attention to human beings, he gave this explanation of what he was doing:

> Then God said, 'Let us make mankind in our image, in our likeness, so that they may rule over the fish in the sea and the birds in the sky, over the livestock and all the wild animals, and over all the creatures that move along the ground.'
>
> So God created mankind in his own image,
>   in the image of God he created them;
>   male and female he created them.
> (Genesis 1:26–7)

Four times in these two verses God says that he is making human beings in his image or likeness.

That is not to say that God looks like a human being. The eternal God is not physical. He does not have hands or feet, eyes or mouth, nor any body part like ours. And yet the Bible frequently describes God as if he does have body parts: God's arm performs his mighty deeds; God's hand is raised in judgement; God speaks face to face with Moses; and all things are laid bare before God's eyes. We find mention of God's feet, God's finger, God's heart, God's nostrils and more. Human body parts are commonly attributed to God, even though he has no body. Why is this?

The counter-intuitive but correct answer is because God is fundamentally *not* like us. He is uncreated; we are created. He is spirit; we are physical. He is infinite; we are finite. Even if we were not imperfect sinners, we would still be restricted in our capacity to understand God because of our human limitations. We can't comprehend the fullness of his majesty, his power or his love, the extent of his infinities. And so, God has to find ways of communicating with us that we can understand, that come within the scope of our abilities. One of the main ways he does this is by using metaphors.

When God created the world, one of his main goals was to show what he is like. He wanted us to know that he is a powerful king, so he created lions. He wanted us to know that he is steadfast and unchanging, so he created rocks. He wanted us to know that he is a provider and a protector, so he created shepherds and sheep. All of the metaphors God uses come from the things he has created precisely for that purpose, so that we can understand him better.

Human bodies were made specifically by God so that he could use them as a metaphor for himself. He wanted us to have arms and hands, faces and eyes, legs and feet, hearts and minds and so on, all so that we could understand more about who he is and what he does. Your body is a living illustration of God himself. As you read the Bible, look out for those metaphors and consider how your own body helps you to know God better.

Human beings are, however, more than bodies, and it is not our bodies that are made in God's image. We are the only part of creation said to be made in his image, and that point is emphasised repeatedly. There must be something special about human beings.

Human beings are different from the rest of creation

I wonder whether you have come across the term 'speciesism'. Those of us who believe that human beings are somehow superior to other animals are called 'speciesist', because we discriminate on the basis of species. Instead, it is argued, animals should have the same moral rights as human beings, and therefore should not be experimented on, kept in captivity, farmed or killed. No species should be discriminated against, in the same way that no group of humans should be discriminated against.

These days many people do believe that human beings are simply another species of animal, with few substantive differences. The recent surge in veganism is partly fuelled by concerns about climate change, but partly by the increasing secularisation of society. If we think of humans simply as one kind of animal, then it makes sense to say that all animals should have the same rights as humans. If the only distinctions we acknowledge are greater intelligence or emotional capacity, then the more scientists discover about animal intelligence and emotions, the smaller the gap between us and the rest of the animal kingdom will become.

But God tells us that human beings really are different. It is amazing to see dogs doing simple arithmetic and elephants showing empathy, but those things are not what sets human beings apart from other species. It doesn't matter how much of our DNA is shared with chimpanzees, the chimpanzee is not made in God's likeness.

When a baby is born, family members like to point out the ways in which the child is like its parents. Perhaps she has her mother's eyes, or he has his father's nose. As the child grows up, the physical resemblance may be joined by similarities of manner, shared talents and other inherited traits. There is no confusion about which is the parent and which is the child, but there can be a strong likeness between them.

In the same way, when God makes human beings in his likeness, it means that we share certain traits with him. It doesn't mean that we are clones of God, and it certainly doesn't mean that we are little gods! And of course we don't have a physical resemblance to God, who is not a physical being at all. So, what do we have in common? There are a number of things, some of which we will come to in later chapters, but here I want to focus on the most important one: love. 'God is love' (1 John 4:8).

That is to say, God is not just capable of loving, but God in himself *is* love. The eternal relationship between the Father, Son and Spirit is a relationship of love. Within himself, therefore, God has always been love. Because we are made in his likeness, we too are made for love.

Try to remember the fiercest, deepest, strongest experience of love you have ever had – perhaps when your first child was born, or when you met your spouse, or when you ran into the safe arms of your mother. That experience of human love gives you a tiny glimpse of what it is like to be God.

Now consider the greatest demonstration of love the world has ever seen. It was made by the one human being who is the precise image of God, the exact representation of his being:

'This is how we know what love is: Jesus Christ laid down his life for us' (1 John 3:16). Christ's self-giving, sacrificial love defines what love is. The one who is perfectly in the image of God is the one who perfectly embodies love.

It is interesting that we're repeatedly told in Genesis 1 that God makes *both* men and women in his likeness. This point is not laboured for other animals, which also come in both male and female versions. I think it's because it is important to understand that men and women *together* are made in God's image. Neither men nor women can claim to reflect adequately the image of God alone. But together, because of our common humanity and our sexed differences, we can reflect something of the way in which the persons of the Godhead relate together in their shared divinity, in love.

Human beings have value because we are in God's likeness

In the previous chapter, we thought about the value we have as human beings because we are made by God. How much more value, then, must we have because we are made like God! We reflect our Creator not merely through his characteristic brushstrokes, but in the very being of ourselves.

All too often these days, people seem to be valued as nothing more than economic tools. What's important is not our health or happiness, but our productivity. School is not so much about educating children as about looking after them so that parents can work long hours to add to the economy. Education itself is primarily a means to a more skilled workforce and therefore a greater GDP. Workers are disposable assets to generate profit for their bosses.

Obviously, it is hard to measure the value of a person objectively, and for some, money is the only way to do it. However, the Bible gives a different perspective on how we measure the value of a person. God's accounting comes in Genesis 9:

And for your lifeblood I will surely demand an accounting. I will demand an accounting from every animal. And from each human being, too, I will demand an accounting for the life of another human being.

'Whoever sheds human blood,
     by humans shall their blood be shed;
for in the image of God
     has God made mankind . . .'
(Genesis 9:5–6)

What is a human being worth? The only thing precious enough to pay the penalty for taking a life is another life. No money, no land, no assets can ever be enough to compensate for shedding human blood, because human beings are made by God in his image.

In Exodus 21, the principle of the death penalty is repeated, and extended to the case of an unborn child.

If people are fighting and hit a pregnant woman and she gives birth prematurely but there is no serious injury, the offender must be fined whatever the woman's husband demands and the court allows. But if there is serious injury, you are to take life for life, eye for eye,

tooth for tooth, hand for hand, foot for foot, burn for
burn, wound for wound, bruise for bruise.
(Exodus 21:22–5)

This passage is not speaking about intentional killing of
unborn children, but about collateral damage as a result of a
fight. The serious injury mentioned is not injury to the woman
but to her child. Whatever damage is done to the unborn child
must be repaid by the one who caused it. If the child is killed,
the death penalty must follow. This is not to be considered an
accidental death, where the killer can escape to a city of refuge
(see Numbers 35:10–12), presumably because the injury is the
result of a deliberate fight, even if the woman and her child
were not the intended victims.

The clear implication of this legislation in Exodus 21 is that
God values the unborn child as highly as he values any other
human being. We should expect that, of course. We know that
God knits us together in our mother's womb, giving us our
personhood from the moment our life begins. We know that
human value doesn't depend on ability, wealth or status. We
know that the unborn child is made in the image of God like
every other human being.

It is desperately sad that in our society unborn children
are intentionally killed in vast numbers. Some 214,869 abor-
tions took place in the UK in 2021. We can't know how many
of those involved twins or more, but perhaps as many as a
quarter of a million people were killed in this way. Legally.

Every one of those was a person, precious because they were
made by God, infinitely valuable because they were made
in the image of God. We don't live in Old Testament Israel,
and I am certainly not advocating for the death penalty for

abortion. For women finding themselves with an unplanned pregnancy, the decision to have an abortion can be agonising, and many suffer with guilt for the rest of their lives. The good news is that the Lord is gracious and merciful, and real forgiveness can be found in this situation.

Assisted suicide and euthanasia remain illegal in the UK, but repeated efforts have been made to change this. As I write, there is a bill awaiting its second hearing in the House of Lords to enable adults who are terminally ill to be provided at their request with specified assistance to end their own lives. A few months ago, at a meeting of the General Synod of the Church of England, we debated a motion concerning assisted suicide, in order to give a clear statement of the Church's position on the subject. An overwhelming majority voted to oppose any form of assisted suicide. But it is telling that the last time General Synod voted on the same subject, they did so unanimously and in 2022 some voted in favour. Our secular society is beginning to forget the value of human life made in God's image, and some Christians are moving the same way as well. But God's valuation holds even at the very end of life, and even in the midst of the deepest suffering. It is not for us to judge the worth of a person on the basis of the quality of their life.

Christ is the model human, being the image of God

If we want to know more about being human, we need to look at the one who is the very image of God. Christ is not only the exact representation of God's being, but also the model for all humanity. When he took on human flesh and blood, he took on our physical limitations: he was subject to the restrictions of created time and space; he needed to sleep and to eat; he experienced pain and grief; he was subject to temptation. 'For we do not have a high priest who is unable to empathize with our weaknesses, but we have one who has been tempted in every way, just as we are – yet he did not sin' (Hebrews 4:15, NIV 2011).

The minutiae of human existence are not glamorous or exciting, no matter how it may appear on some people's Instagram feed. The routines of cleaning, cooking, eating, working and sleeping never stop. The process of ageing can't be halted or reversed, whatever the latest beauty treatments may tell us. Daily interactions with other people are an endless source of potential frustration and irritation. There is no smooth path through life. And if there were for Christ, he certainly did not take it.

The Gospel writers did not record all the details of Christ's normal human experiences. No biographies or biopics of other people include all of those details either. We can just assume that they slept and got dressed and went to the toilet and so on. But it is an extraordinary truth of the incarnation to consider that Christ did all of those mundane activities, just like you and I.

He lived a normal life, *yet he did not sin*. Christ's life demonstrates an extremely important aspect of our humanity: sin is not part of it. Sin is the universal experience of all human beings except Christ, but Christ shows us that it is possible to be fully human and yet not sin. Sin is an aberration in our humanity, not a necessary part of it.

Even though he experienced all the frustrations of daily life, Christ did not lie, gossip, lose his temper, complain or envy.

Even when he was tired and hungry, he was patient, kind, compassionate and forgiving. In his humanity, he nevertheless lived a life of perfect godliness. 'When they hurled their insults at him, he did not retaliate; when he suffered, he made no threats. Instead, he entrusted himself to him who judges justly' (1 Peter 2:23).

This is how a human being, made in the image of God, lives in accordance with his true humanity. This is the model for all of us.

Questions to consider

1 Genesis 1:27 tells us that human beings are created in God's likeness. In what ways are human beings like God? And in what ways are we unlike God?
2 Why does God create both men and women to be in his image? What does this reflect about God that one sex alone could not?
3 Who are the people least valued in our society and our world? Why are these people (along with everyone else) so precious to God?
4 What changes could individuals, churches or governments make to show that every person is valuable?
5 What can we learn about being human from Christ's human life?

3

Being human means being men and women

So God created mankind in his own image,
   in the image of God he created them;
   male and female he created them.
(Genesis 1:27)

In the summer following my first year at university I received a letter from my college, informing me that the bursar previously known as Simon Stone would from now on be called Susan Marshall. The next day, this story was on the front page of the *Daily Mail*. That was my first encounter with what we now call transgender. Back in 1992, it didn't occur to any of us students to question what it meant to be a man or a woman, or whether it was possible to change. We all assumed we already knew the answer to that: whatever the bursar decided to wear or wanted to be called, he remained a man.

Thirty years later, a story like this wouldn't even rate a small paragraph in the back pages of a national newspaper. Middle-aged men and neurodivergent teenagers are announcing that they are transgender at unprecedented rates.[1] Forms frequently

---

1 '44% of trans women who responded to the survey started transitioning by the age of 24, compared with 84% of trans men': <www.gov.uk/government/publications/national-lgbt-survey-summary-report/national-lgbt-survey-summary-report> (accessed 10 February 2023). Helen Joyce, in her book *Trans: When ideology meets reality*, states: 'In 1989, when the Tavistock clinic opened, there were two referrals, both young boys. By 2020, there were 2,378 referrals, almost three-quarters of them girls, and most of those teenagers' (London: Oneworld, 2021, p. 101). A study of teenagers identifying as

ask us to state whether our gender is male, female or other. Politicians tie themselves into knots trying to answer the question of what a woman is in a way that is both honest and 'woke'. Children and teenagers with various mental health problems are routinely asked if they are transgender, as if addressing that alone will solve their other issues.

And so, the statement in Genesis 1:27 that God made us male and female is more important than ever. The debate about sex and gender affects not only a few individuals but all human beings. What does it mean that we are made male and female, and why does it matter?

Men and women

But for Adam no suitable helper was found. So the LORD God caused the man to fall into a deep sleep; and while he was sleeping, he took one of the man's ribs and then closed up the place with flesh. Then the LORD God made a woman from the rib he had taken out of the man, and he brought her to the man. The man said,

'This is now bone of my bones
    and flesh of my flesh;
she shall be called "woman",
    for she was taken out of man.'

That is why a man leaves his father and mother and is united to his wife, and they become one flesh.
(Genesis 2:20–4)

---

transgender found high rates of correlation with a diagnosis of autism: <https://pubmed.ncbi.nlm.nih.gov/32770077/> (accessed 10 February 2023).

Men and women have different bodies. We have different chromosomes, different hormones and different genitalia. We also, of course, have bodies that share almost every other feature in common. The creation account in Genesis 2 shows us Eve being formed out of Adam's rib to demonstrate that she is made of exactly the same stuff as he is made from. To be male or female is also to be human.

After she has been made, Eve is brought to Adam by God, and together they form the first family unit. They set the example for every subsequent family, in which a man and a woman come together, leaving their family homes, to establish a new household. This is something that neither could do on their own, since it involves sexual union and establishes the context in which children can be born and raised. We're also shown that men and women were created to work together: both are given the responsibilities of ruling and subduing the earth (Genesis 1:28), and Eve was made to be a helper, working alongside Adam in his work of tending the garden.[2]

Our physical differences are one way of defining our sex: men are human beings with male bodies and women are human beings with female bodies. But identifying those bodily differences is not enough; we also need to ask *why* God makes us different. God has a purpose in humanity being made male and female: men and women were created by God to work together and to live together. We were designed to help each other and to love each other.

One way we human beings fulfil our role as a living visual aid for God is in acting out the story of salvation through

2 Elsewhere in the Old Testament it is God who takes this 'helper' role (e.g. Deuteronomy 33:29; Psalm 118:7), therefore we shouldn't assume that it implies Eve has a lesser status than Adam here.

marriage. Throughout the Bible, God's relationship to his people is described in romantic terms: a courtship, a betrothal and a marriage, sadly followed by betrayal, adultery and prostitution, ending with divorce and then, wonderfully, restoration. In the Old Testament, this imagery is explicitly used in several of the prophetic books (Isaiah, Jeremiah, Ezekiel and Hosea), as well as in the Song of Songs. Christ frequently refers to himself in parables as a bridegroom. Paul famously builds on the metaphor in Ephesians 5, and then the book of Revelation brings the whole of Scripture to a climax with its vision of the future consummation of this wedding between the Lamb and his Church.

> Then I saw 'a new heaven and a new earth,' for the first heaven and the first earth had passed away, and there was no longer any sea. I saw the Holy City, the new Jerusalem, coming down out of heaven from God, prepared as a bride beautifully dressed for her husband. (Revelation 21:1–2)

This relationship is not symmetrical. The bride and the bridegroom do not have interchangeable roles. The church cannot be the redeemer; Christ is not the one who is redeemed. So, when God designed men and women to have the kind of relationship that would help us to understand this plan of salvation, he did not make them interchangeable either. He made men to be modelled after Christ and women to be modelled after the Church.

A biblical definition of a man might be something like: 'A man is a person who, in marriage, must love his wife sacrificially, laying down his life for her, in order to help us understand something of how Christ sacrificially loves his bride, the Church.' If you are a man, this is your role whether it comes naturally or has to be undertaken consciously. Where your own needs clash with your wife's, you are to sacrifice yourself. Where you are physically stronger than her, you are to protect her. Where you can serve her, you must do so. Lay down your life for her, so that we can all feel just how much it cost Christ to lay down his life for all of us.

A man who is not married is still a man, of course. Christ himself was not married, and yet he was our model human being and specifically the model for manhood. In his single state he embodied this self-sacrificial love and showed tender care for those who were vulnerable and needy, including women. You can fulfil your God-given masculinity without marriage and without sex in the way that you follow Christ's own example.

A matching biblical definition of a woman could be: 'A woman is a person who, in marriage, is sacrificially loved by her husband. She joyfully submits herself to her husband, knowing and trusting that his love for her will be for their mutual good, in order that we will understand how we should respond to Christ in joyful submission and trust.' If you are a woman, this is your role whether it comes naturally or has to be undertaken consciously. You will seek to please your husband in faithful obedience, working alongside him and trusting him to provide for you.

A woman who is not married can fulfil her God-given femininity without marriage and without sex, by demonstrating this response of faithful obedience and submission to Christ, which will be seen in the way she loves and cares for others.

In God's creation designs, human maleness and femaleness are not arbitrary or irrelevant. They are not limited to body parts or sexual function. God made you a man or a woman for a purpose, so that you could play your part in this story of revelation and salvation. He made men and women to be distinct and different, just as Christ and the Church are distinct and different. But God also made men and women to share a common humanity, just as the persons of God share a common divinity.

Human sex matters to God. It is not interchangeable or transferable. It is not simply a question of individual identity but one of eternal salvation.

The problem of gender

While it is important to say clearly that God creates us as men and women, it is true that a very small number of people are born with overlapping male and female physical characteristics.[3] Intersex people may have a combination of male chromosomes with female genitalia, or vice versa, or may have a combination of both male and female genitalia. For most of these people, it is still very obvious whether they are a man or a woman, despite their intersex condition. Intersex, like all physical frailties, is a result of the broken world we all live in following the fall, not a consequence of any individual's sin. It often causes infertility

---

3 While some people quote a statistic of around 1.7% of the population, this is based on false inclusion of many conditions that are not usually considered as intersex. The actual number is around 0.018%. See: <www.leonardsax.com/how-common-is-intersex-a-response-to-anne-fausto-sterling/> (accessed 10 February 2023).

and may be linked to other medical problems.[4] Intersex is not part of the world in Genesis 1 and 2, and intersex people will have their sex restored and redeemed in the new creation.

While intersex conditions have existed throughout human history since the fall, transgender as it is understood now is a much more recent phenomenon. A widely reported poll from 2015 indicated that 50% of American millennials (born between 1981 and 1997) thought that gender existed on a spectrum, rather than in fixed categories. This might be expressed as being 'non-binary' or 'genderqueer', and by using pronouns such as they/them, zie/hir or per/pers.

A transgender person has no sexual discrepancy between their hormones, chromosomes and genitalia: their bodies are unambiguously male or female. However, they experience strong internal feelings that they *ought* to be the other sex, or even that they *are* the other sex. These feelings are given priority over the objective reality of their bodily sex, and they choose to present themselves as if they belong to the opposite sex – by using an alternative name and opposite pronouns, and by altering their appearance.

Gender dysphoria is the psychological condition of having a disconnect between physical sex and internal sense of gender. In these cases, the desire to conform their body to their perceived gender can be strong enough to undergo surgery and to receive hormone treatments, even knowing that they are likely to lead to permanent infertility and

---

4 A study of intersex people in the USA found high levels of depression, anxiety, arthritis and hypertension. Nearly a third of those surveyed had difficulty with everyday tasks and over half reported serious difficulties with cognitive tasks. See: <www.ncbi.nlm. nih.gov/pmc/articles/PMC7546494/> (accessed 10 February 2023).

increased risk of other life-threatening conditions.[5] Someone suffering with gender dysphoria is likely to be extremely unhappy and at risk of other mental health disorders. The answer is not, however, to try to conform their body to their desired sex. This is a strategy that could only ever have limited success since the physical differences between men and women are too extensive to be reversed by surgery or medical treatment. But even if it were possible, it would not be kind and it would not be honouring to God. Instead, we need to recognise this as a genuine psychiatric disorder and treat it appropriately, with compassion, helping the person to accept who they are in the body God has made for them.

Many transgender people express their feelings of being a different gender from their sex in terms of not fitting in to societal norms: boys who enjoy playing with dolls or dressing up; girls who like climbing trees and getting muddy. Ironically, identifying gender in this way relies on extremely strong, old-fashioned gender stereotypes that the feminist movement of the past fifty years has worked hard to destroy. When I was at school in the 1980s we were repeatedly told that women could do anything men do. We could be astronauts or explorers, engineers or bankers. We could spend our leisure hours playing sport, drinking in pubs or using power tools. The world was open to us as women. We did not need to be men to be like men, or to identify as men in order to succeed in any field or enjoy any activity. Of course not. Those things do not define our gender. God did not design men to watch football and women to go shopping.

---

5 Cross-sex hormones are associated with increased risk of heart attack, stroke, dementia, liver disease, diabetes and other conditions for transmen. For transwomen, there is evidence that they cause fatigue, brittle bones, raised cholesterol levels and increased risk of some cancers. For more information, see Joyce, *Trans*, p. 91.

Gender stereotypes are not limited to skills and activities, but also include character and personality. Women, we're told, are more nurturing, more emotional, more compassionate, kinder and gentler. Men, by contrast, are stronger, braver, more natural leaders, more aggressive and more self-reliant. The stereotypes have some basis in reality, but it is a matter of debate how much they are the result of nature or of nurture. Are men born to be more aggressive, or do boys learn to be more aggressive through the way they are raised? Are women naturally more compassionate, or are girls taught to be so as they grow up?

Whether these are innate or learned traits, they are by no means restricted to people of one sex or the other. There are plenty of kind, compassionate and gentle men, as well as many strong, brave women who are natural leaders. Stereotypes are not a good way to define gender, and an insistence on conformity to these stereotypes may end up having the unintended consequence of causing more people to question their gender.

As Christians, we must look to God rather than to our unreliable feelings or our contemporary secular society in order to find our identity. We are, first and foremost, human beings made in God's image, to reflect his likeness and to demonstrate his saving love. We are men and women, as demonstrated in our physical bodies and defined by God's purposes in creation and revelation. Unlike the unstable shifting sands of gender identity, these are concrete realities.

As we navigate these complicated issues it can be hard for us to know how to respond to our own bodies and our own feelings. Teenagers going through all the physical and hormonal changes of puberty are particularly susceptible to the idea of something that could explain the feeling of being uncomfortable in their own bodies. It is normal to question our sexuality and identity, and we need to be patient and gentle with ourselves and others going through this process.

Questions to consider
1 Why is it important that God made both men and women?
2 What does it mean that you are a man or a woman? Why did God choose to give you that sex?
3 How can men and women reflect God's purpose for them as they work together, worship together and build families together?
4 What is the difference between the Bible's understanding of men and women, and that of secular society today?
5 How should Christians respond to people who identify as transgender or non-binary?

4

Being human means being made for work

I wonder whether you've ever done the kind of thought experiment where you suddenly come into an enormous sum of money. Perhaps a long-lost relative leaves you unimagined wealth in their will, or you pick up a winning Euromillions lottery ticket in the supermarket car park. If you were in a situation where you did not need to work in order to pay bills or put food on the table, and had financial freedom to make any choices, what would you choose to do with your life?

For most of us, of course, there is no choice. Either we must work because we need the money, or we cannot work due to age, health or other responsibilities. The introduction of the state pension in the UK in 1909 heralded the arrival of retirement as a significant part of most people's lives. Now, we all expect to be able to stop work at some point and enjoy perhaps twenty or thirty years of leisure. The underlying assumption behind this attitude is that work is what gets in the way of enjoying life. Work is a necessary evil, to be got out of the way as soon as possible.

It is striking, isn't it, how many lottery winners find that sudden wealth does not bring the happiness they expected? Indeed, Sudden Wealth Syndrome is a well-documented phenomenon, including depression, paranoia, guilt and an inability to make decisions. Some lottery winners end up wasting vast sums of money and within a few years are back at work. Wealth is not an unalloyed good, and work is certainly not a 'necessary evil'. It is a key part of God's good creation.

Good work

We know that we are made in God's image and that this has all kinds of profound implications. But it makes sense to begin by looking at the immediate context of that statement to see what God is like. And at the beginning of Genesis 2 we find a surprising aspect to that likeness:

> By the seventh day God had finished the work he had been doing; so on the seventh day he rested from all his work. Then God blessed the seventh day and made it holy, because on it he rested from all the work of creating that he had done.
> (Genesis 2:2–3)

What is God doing in Genesis 1 and 2? He is creating. He is doing the work of creating. God is a worker. Work cannot be a bad thing, since God undertakes work.

I think it is important to state clearly here that throughout this chapter I am using a much broader definition of 'work' than merely 'paid work'. God was not paid to make the heavens and the earth! Adam was not paid to work the land in the garden of Eden. Work in this broader sense could be defined as something like: 'Activity undertaken intentionally and diligently for the benefit of oneself and others.'

Paid work certainly fits this definition. Whatever you are doing in a job, it should be done intentionally and diligently.

And because it benefits others, you receive a wage for it. But all kinds of other things are encompassed in this view of work as well: raising a family, caring for an elderly relative, volunteering for a church or a charity, organising community events, praying faithfully. Construed in this way, work becomes something that gives a purpose and a structure to our lives, just as it did for God, who worked for six days and then rested on the seventh. Working and then resting is a God-given and God-imitating pattern for human life.

Not all people can be workers. For some people, health issues prevent them from undertaking any kind of work, paid or unpaid. Young children are not workers. For most of us, however, during most of our lives, we should be engaged in some kind of activity undertaken intentionally and diligently for the benefit of ourselves and others. We each have different inherent capacity for work, and different skills and circumstances governing the kinds of work we can do. But none of us is designed by God for a life of idle leisure.

Working for the world

God blessed them and said to them, 'Be fruitful and increase in number; fill the earth and subdue it. Rule over the fish in the sea and the birds in the sky and over every living creature that moves on the ground.'
(Genesis 1:28)

In the whole account of creation, this is a unique moment, where God speaks to what he has created and tells them what he has created them for. Birds and animals, plants and trees, the sun and the seas – they don't need telling. They just do what they do. But human beings are made in God's image, with consciousness and intelligence, and they are told what God's purpose is for them.

They are to be fruitful and increase in number. Humans are made for families, to reproduce, to spread across the whole earth, so that humans can subdue the whole earth. We are to rule over the rest of creation. We are put in this place of authority by God himself, from whom all authority is derived. It is an awesome responsibility and it will not be fulfilled by living idly.

Our purpose is to organise, to steward, to care for, to tend and to tame the world. While all species have an impact on the environment, it is only human beings who can do so consciously. For example, cows will always produce methane. They don't think about that or attempt to regulate it, but humans can control the cattle population to determine the overall level of methane produced. Some animals can take items from their surroundings and modify them to use as tools in collecting food, but humans can make informed decisions about where and how much to mine for minerals or drill for oil, and how to minimise the impact of this on the environment. Animals may notice when it gets harder to find food or a suitable mate, but humans can identify species that are endangered and take active steps to rebuild a population to sustainable levels. We can see the impact of our activity on different ecosystems and find ways to reverse those effects.

God makes us in his image so that we can work in this sort of way: creatively problem-solving, seeing the bigger picture. We don't have the same capacity as God who creates from nothing and can see all eternity, but we can think beyond our immediate situation. We can imagine different ways of doing things and what might be the outcomes. We are made in God's image to work, and we are made to work in God's image.

Not all of us will engage in paid work that relates directly to this kind of stewarding of creation, but we all participate in some kind of relationship with the environment. It is work to separate our recycling from our rubbish, or to wash cloth nappies rather than throw out disposable ones every time. Part of our work is to consider how we want to exercise our God-given responsibilities to fill and subdue the earth. For many of us, this will include considering how we use the income from our work to support others who are more directly involved in stewarding creation.

Working for our own needs

The LORD God took the man and put him in the Garden of Eden to work it and take care of it. And the LORD God commanded the man, 'You are free to eat from any tree in the garden . . .'
(Genesis 2:15–16)

The general instruction to rule the earth in Genesis 1 is repeated in the specific setting of Genesis 2: this particular man is to take care of this particular part of the earth. Adam must work the land but not exploit it. He must take care of the land, and in return the land will provide for him.

This pattern of working in order to provide for the needs of oneself and one's family is repeated throughout the Bible. The proverbs are scathing about those who are too idle to work:

A sluggard's appetite is never filled,
 but the desires of the diligent are fully satisfied.
(Proverbs 13:4)

All hard work brings a profit,
 but mere talk leads only to poverty.
(Proverbs 14:23)

Paul reiterates this point for the benefit of the Thessalonian Christians who had thought they no longer needed to work:

For even when we were with you, we gave you this rule: 'The one who is unwilling to work shall not eat.' We hear that some among you are idle and disruptive. They are not busy; they are busybodies. Such people we command and urge in the Lord Jesus Christ to settle down and earn the food they eat.
(2 Thessalonians 3:10–12)

Christian generosity to the poor was never meant to be abused by those who could and should work for their own living. Work is a good thing, in which we follow God's own example, and through which we can provide for ourselves and our families.

For some people, work is not the way they provide for their own needs. Whether they are independently wealthy, or living on a pension or benefits, paid work is not possible or necessary. But even in these situations, it is not good for us to be idle. We all need a purpose. We need to find a way of working for the benefit of others. I recently read about a housebound older lady who found her purpose and structure in praying for the world. Every day she would take the newspaper and begin by praying for those in the headline stories, the politicians and world leaders. Then she would turn to the obituaries and pray for all those who had been bereaved. She prayed for the people whose weddings were announced and the families of the children newly born. Finally, she prayed for her own family, friends, acquaintances and community, before ending by thanking God for all his blessings in her own life. That lady was a worker![1]

By contrast, I heard a sobering story a few days ago, about a couple who, unable to have children, worked hard, retired early, built their dream home – and both died within ten years from alcohol-related diseases. They could buy anything they wanted, but they drank themselves to death because they had no purpose in their lives. They did not need paid work to provide for their needs, but they needed something more than endless leisure in order to live satisfying lives.

Work is a good thing, given to us by God for our benefit. But it is not a good thing when it becomes a goal in its own right, and one important way to follow God's model of work is by resting. After God spent six days working to create the universe, he rested on the seventh day. In so doing, he established the pattern for human work, which should also include regular rest:

> Remember the Sabbath day by keeping it holy. Six days you shall labour and do all your work, but the seventh day is a sabbath to the LORD your God. On it you shall

---

[1] This story is told in more detail in David Crump, *Knocking on Heaven's Door: A New Testament theology of petitionary prayer*, (Grand Rapids, MI: Baker Academic, 2006), pp. 245–46.

not do any work, neither you, nor your son or daughter, nor your male or female servant, nor your animals, nor any foreigner residing in your towns. For in six days the LORD made the heavens and the earth, the sea, and all that is in them, but he rested on the seventh day. Therefore the LORD blessed the Sabbath day and made it holy.
(Exodus 20:8–11)

For the ancient Israelites wandering in the wilderness, the Sabbath day was an act of faith. Would God really provide enough for them to get through this day? When they settled in the land, it continued to require faith. If the harvest was ready on the Sabbath day, could they trust the Lord that it would still be there the next day? What if a storm came and destroyed the crop? The Sabbath year, of course, was an even greater test of their faith. How could they survive for a whole year without working the land that provided for their needs? It was supposed to be a reminder that, although their hard work brought profit, in the end it was God who provided for them.

We are still the same created human beings who need to follow God's model of work and rest. We cannot continue to work without adequate rest for too long before we burn out. We need to learn how to trust God to provide for us, even when we are not working every waking moment. Look at the scope of the rest envisaged in Exodus 20 again: this is not just about hard agricultural labour. No one is to work. No chores are to be done. No cleaning, no housework, not even by the servants. Of course, we know that some works of mercy and necessity must be done, even on rest days. Children must be fed, clothed and cleaned. Caring work must continue. Animals must be fed and looked after. But if your days off are crammed full with non-paid work, I think you may need to reconsider how you are spending your time in order to incorporate more rest.

During the pandemic, when many activities necessarily had to be paused, a lot of people noticed how much better it was to have more time in their week for rest. People found joy in going for long walks, playing games with the family or enjoying movie nights together rather than rushing around after school to drop one child at Brownies, collect another from football, and cobble together a World Book Day costume for the third. Inevitably, that slower pace of life did not last long after the lockdowns ended. Yet perhaps it should have. Perhaps we really are all doing too much.

Take a moment to think about how many hours each week you spend on work activities, whether paid or unpaid. And then think about when you rest. Are you following God's model of work and rest, so that your rest enables you to work to your best ability? What changes might you need to make?

Working in a fallen world

While work is a good part of God's good creation, we need to recognise that the nature of work has been impacted greatly by sin. God's curse on Adam explicitly made his work hard and frustrating. I am sure many of us can testify from our own experiences of work that it is hard and frustrating! I don't mean to say in this chapter that we should be channelling an inner Pollyanna in order to take delight in every boring, exhausting, irritating part of our work. For most of us, paid work will be the means to the end of providing for our families and ourselves, and unpaid work will be the means to the end of caring for our families and ourselves. That makes it worthwhile, no matter what the actual tasks are.

In the New Testament world, slaves worked at the whim of their masters, unable to refuse, no matter how hard, miserable, frustrating or tedious the task. Paul tells Christian slaves that even in this situation, the way they do their work is important to the Lord:

> Slaves, obey your earthly masters in everything; and do it, not only when their eye is on you and to curry their favour, but with sincerity of heart and reverence for the Lord. Whatever you do, work at it with all your heart, as working for the Lord, not for human masters, since you know that you will receive an inheritance from the Lord as a reward. It is the Lord Christ you are serving. (Colossians 3:22–4)

This is true for all of us. Whether you are scrubbing vomit out of a car seat or praying through the newspaper; whether you are delivering pizzas or Amazon parcels; whether you are volunteering at your local school or at church: *whatever* you are doing, work at it with all your heart. If you are running your own business, if you are self-employed, or if you are a senior manager in your workplace, remember that you too are working for the Lord, and do it wholeheartedly.

God sees our work and values it, not just for what we do but how we do it. He sees how we bear the boredom with patience, the frustration with graciousness, the repetitiveness with perseverance. He sees how we use our influence for the good of others, how we fulfil our responsibilities diligently and how we care for those we supervise.

And he will reward us accordingly.

Questions to consider

1 Are you surprised to find that work is presented so positively in the Bible? What are the reasons we're given to show that work is a good thing?
2 Why is it that work doesn't always feel like a good thing?
3 Look again at the verses from Colossians 3. What difference would it make if you had this attitude to your work?
4 What is the pattern of work and rest established in the Bible? Why do you think God gives us this pattern?
5 What practical changes could you make to have a more godly pattern of work and rest in your life?

5

Being human means being both body and soul

Then the LORD God formed a man from the dust of the ground and breathed into his nostrils the breath of life, and the man became a living being.
(Genesis 2:7)

In Genesis 1 we're told about how God created humanity as a whole, but here in Genesis 2 the focus narrows to the creation of the first person. The man is formed from the dust of the ground; that is to say he is made from the same stuff as the rest of creation. When the woman is made later, from his rib, one of the things this tells us is that she is made from exactly the same stuff he is. All people, men and women alike, are made as part of the physical universe in which we live. We know this to be true scientifically: our bodies are made of atoms and molecules that may once have existed in trees, or the ocean, or even as dust on the ground. It is also true theologically: human beings are part of God's creation, not separate from it.

The creation of Adam does not stop with his physical body. Once the body is formed, God breathes life into it. It is as if the body is a clay sculpture that only comes to life when it is filled with God's breath, or with God's spirit (the original Hebrew word used can mean either). Human beings are not merely physical creatures. We are a union of body and spirit.

Throughout the Bible, this understanding of humanity is expressed especially with respect to death, which is described as the separation of body and soul (see Ecclesiastes 12:7 and James 2:26). At death, our bodies return to the ground, and decay into their constituent elements. But our souls are held, in paradise or in Sheol,[1] until the great day of resurrection, when bodies and souls will be reunited into eternal life or eternal destruction.

In our secular society, some people have moved towards the notion that we are simply bodies, nothing but animals with a greater level of intelligence but not qualitatively different from them. Others have moved in the opposite direction, identifying our humanity in the brain. In this view, bodies are simply glorified jars to hold our brains. Or perhaps they are soft, warm biological computer towers, hosting more RAM than we know what to do with?

The Bible does not allow us to fall into this dichotomy, valuing brains over bodies, identifying with our inner being and dismissing our external reality. Our bodies are us, but we are also more than our bodies.

Our bodies are us

Take a look in the mirror – a full-length mirror, so you can see your whole body. You are unique in your appearance, even if you have an identical twin. Your hair, your eyes, your smile, your muscular arms or wide hips, that scar from a childhood

---

1 The Bible uses different words for these temporary resting-places of the soul from those it uses for the eternal states of the reunited body and soul. Paradise is where, for example, the thief on the cross went after his death (Luke 23:43). Sheol is where the psalmist fears going in death (e.g. Psalms 89:48; 116:3).

accident, that birthmark. Your body is your own, not a copy of anyone else's. Your body is a result of your specific DNA, but it is also a result of your particular life history: what you have eaten, what sports you have played, what surgery you've needed, what choices you've made about piercings or tattoos. Your body is a physical statement of you and your life.

Your body has an impact on everything you do in life: how fast you walk, how much you can carry, whether you can breastfeed your child. Your hormones impact your emotional mood, but so does physical pain. It's hard to be patient and kind when you've got unbearable toothache. It's even harder when you have a chronic condition that means you are in pain day after day without any respite.

Your body includes your brain. Brains are not separate, non-physical organs that operate independently of our bodies. Your brain is made up of cells like the rest of your body. Every thought you have occurs within the network of physical neurotransmitters in your brain. Memory, feelings, senses and thoughts are all physically enacted in your brain structures. No wonder scientists still have little idea about much of the human brain's function! It is massive and complex, much more so than even the largest super-computers. But it is a physical organ. You can take it out and put it in a jar and touch it, though I don't recommend it!

You do not exist without the body God created for you to have. When he knit you together in your mother's womb, he planned out your physical appearance and your bodily functions. He knew whether you would have a disability or abnormality. He knew whether you would become a fast runner or a brilliant musician. He gave you the body you have in order to fulfil the plans he has for you.

Next time you look in the mirror, then, thank God, who made your body. Thank him for your spleen and your pancreas (and if you need to, look up what they do and why you need them). Thank him for the blood pumping around your body and the oxygen absorbed by your lungs. Praise God for your eyes and ears, to see and hear the world around you. Think about the parts of your body you wish were different in some way, and try to thank God for those too.

A few months ago, in the middle of a friendly, if cautious, conversation with some non-Christian friends about gender identity, one of them said: 'I am who I am despite my body.'

For me, it was an eye-opening moment in understanding some of the baffling transgender ideology that I was struggling to grasp. Because, you see, what she was saying is that her body was not *her*. It was not even part of her. As she saw it, her body was a separate thing, merely a complex case in which to house her real self. This separation of the body from the self is not a new idea. Descartes famously located human identity in human thought: 'I think, therefore I am.' He claimed that our existence can be proved by our consciousness of it. If our identity is located in and proved by our thought, as he held, what value do our bodies have?

Some Christians have followed a similar line of thought, denying that the body has any value and thus turning to lives of extreme asceticism, including celibacy, fasting and poverty. Taking this one step further, others have identified the body as the location of sin, and thus practised self-inflicted pain in order to grow in sanctification. Neither of these views is biblical![2] 'Has not the one God made you? You belong to him in body and spirit' (Malachi 2:15). God made people, not merely spirits. We belong to him in both body and spirit, because we belong to him as whole persons. Here, the prophet is pronouncing God's judgement on the priests who have failed in their duties because of their adultery. What they have done with their bodies makes them unfit to serve God in body or spirit.

Paul makes exactly the same point in 1 Corinthians:

> Do you not know that your bodies are members of Christ himself? Shall I then take the members of Christ and unite them with a prostitute? Never! Do you not know that he who unites himself with a prostitute is one with her in body? For it is said, 'The two will become one flesh.' But whoever is united with the Lord is one with him in spirit. Flee from sexual immorality. All other sins a person commits are outside the body, but whoever sins sexually, sins against their own body. Do you not know that your bodies are temples of the Holy Spirit, who is in you, whom you have received from God? You are not your own; you were bought at a price. Therefore honour God with your bodies.
> (1 Corinthians 6:15–20)

Our bodies are members of Christ himself, Paul says. When we talk about being 'in Christ' I think we often assume this is

---

2 This second view comes from a wrong understanding of the term 'flesh' in the New Testament. When Paul talks about 'flesh', for example in Romans 8:1–8, he does not mean the physical body by contrast with the soul. He is talking about our sinful nature, both body and soul.

true in some disembodied, spiritual way. But Paul is absolutely clear that, if we are in Christ, that refers to our whole person, including our body. What we do with our bodies matters because our bodies are united with Christ and our bodies are temples for the Holy Spirit.

Your body is not separate from you. Christ does not save 'you' without your body. He saves *all* of you. You – and therefore your body – are united to Christ. You – and therefore your body – must honour God.

Bodies are extraordinary things. They are complex biological organisms that are constantly undertaking all kinds of vital functions without any conscious instruction. Right now, your kidneys are filtering out waste, your arteries are carrying blood to every inch of you, your spleen is doing whatever it is that spleens do . . . and you don't even notice. Your brain is firing synapses off left and right to keep you alert and help you to make sense of what you are reading, but it is simultaneously regulating your body temperature and reminding you to breathe.

Our bodies are all subject to limitations. We can only be in one place at one time. We have a maximum processing speed and a maximum moving speed (and, for some of us, those are quite low!). We may have particular limitations due to disability or disease. We may become more conscious of limitations restricting our capacity as we grow older. These limitations are not a bad thing. God did not intend us to be able to do all things in all places at all times! Indeed, the physical limitations of our bodies are a tangible daily reminder that we are not God and that we depend on God.

You might want your body to be different from the way it is now, and there are some things you can do to change it. You could undertake a physical exercise programme designed to make you faster and stronger. You could introduce dietary changes to ensure that you have a better intake of vitamins and minerals, and a better balance of protein, fibre, fat and carbohydrate. That could help you either gain weight or lose it. I am not good at putting these things into practice, but I do think we should honour God with our bodies by taking good care of them physically. We can serve God better when we are healthier, and most people can take some steps towards being healthier.

We need to be careful not to let better health or 'better bodies' become idols, however. Obsessive weight control and excessive exercise are not honouring to God if they are a sign that we are putting our bodies in the place of God. Addiction to cosmetic surgery or tattoos can be another indication of this wrong priority. Reconstructive surgery following severe burns or a mastectomy may be very important, but simply trying to conform to a particular ideal of beauty is not. Honour God with the body he has given you, not by conforming that body to a false ideal of beauty.

Your body has been created and redeemed by God. It is united with Christ and a temple for the Spirit. Your body matters, and what you do with it matters. Your body is you.

You are more than your body

Your body is you, but you are more than your body. In the Bible, three aspects of a human being are mentioned: the body, the spirit and the soul (see 1 Thessalonians 5:23). It is hard to draw out precisely the difference between spirit and soul, and the terms are used slightly differently in the Old and New Testaments.

In the Old Testament, the spirit (or the breath) is what God breathes into a body to give it life. The spirit is the difference between a body and a person. The Hebrew word for spirit is *ruach*. The Hebrew word sometimes translated as soul is *nephesh*. A better translation might be 'a life', or 'a person'. When we talk about the number of souls drowned on the *Titanic*, that is the sense in which *nephesh* means soul. It is the life of the person, everything they are. Repeatedly, we're instructed to love the Lord with all our heart, strength and soul; that is, with every fibre of our being.

In the New Testament, the spirit (or the breath) is what God breathes into a body to give it life, and it is also what God breathes into a person to give them new life. The Greek word for spirit is *pneuma*, and like *ruach* it can also mean breath or wind. When Jesus died, he gave up his spirit, his *pneuma* (Matthew 27:50). The Greek word translated soul is *psyche*, and it has the sense of the inner being, the seat of emotion, intelligence and personality.

While the terminology is a bit complicated with these various overlapping ideas, it is clear that the Bible consistently shows human beings to be more than their physical bodies. There is something beyond our physical existence and it is something that matters very much indeed. Our lives, our personhood, our identity and our eternal existence don't exist without our bodies, but they extend far beyond our bodies. There is something about us that is not limited to the neurotransmissions of a physical brain, or the hormonal surges of a physical endocrine system. There is a spirit or a soul, there is a life.

A couple of years ago, I witnessed the progressive physical decline of a friend of mine who had motor neurone disease. By the last time I saw her, just before the first Covid lockdown, she could barely speak, she was struggling to eat and she had no other movement. And yet, everything about her lit up when I arrived with another friend, to look at the Bible and pray together. It was a privilege to witness the exponential growth in her faith, hope and joy that accompanied the increasing failures of her body. She was always more than her body, as we all are, but it was never more evident than in those last months of her life.

We all have an inner life, an inner being, a part of us that is not separate from our body but is more than our body. It is where we feel and think, where we imagine and dream. It is both the source of our sin and the home of the Holy Spirit. It is where our sinful words and deeds emerge from, and where the fruits of the Spirit grow. In Matthew, Jesus calls this the heart: 'But the things that come out of a person's mouth come from the heart, and these defile them. For out of the heart come evil thoughts – murder, adultery, sexual immorality, theft, false testimony, slander' (Matthew 15:18–19).

Our body is not what causes us to sin, but our inner being causes our body to sin. Our heart, our soul, our spirit – all these are infected by sin and give rise to the sins we commit in our body. Our inner being is more powerful than our physical body, controlling what we do with our body. Therefore, we must give even greater attention to our inner being than we do to our outer body.

'What good will it be for someone to gain the whole world, yet forfeit their soul? Or what can anyone give in exchange for their soul?' (Matthew 16:26). There is nothing on earth worth exchanging for your soul. No wealth, no status, no adrenaline rush, no prize. There is nothing you can give to buy your soul back once lost. You are more valuable than everything else put together. So take care of your precious soul. Entrust it to Christ, who will hold on to it more securely than you could manage yourself.

Your body matters to the Lord, but your soul matters even more.

Questions to consider

1 Why do you think God gave you the body that you have? How could you do better at caring for your body and honouring it as God's creation?

2 How do the limitations of your body help you to depend on God more?

3 Deuteronomy 8:3 says, 'He humbled you, causing you to hunger and then feeding you with manna, which neither you nor your ancestors had known, to teach you that man does not live on bread alone but on every word that comes from the mouth of the LORD.' How should we take care of our souls just as we take care of our bodies? How are the two linked?

4 As you look forward to the new creation when you will be renewed, body and soul, what are you most excited about? If you need some inspiration, look at Isaiah 35:5–10 or 1 Corinthians 15:42–4.

6

Being human means being with others

The LORD God said, 'It is not good for the man to be alone. I will make a helper suitable for him.'
(Genesis 2:18)

In those first moments in the garden, Adam was surrounded by birds and animals of all kinds. He was living in a beautiful landscape of rivers and trees. He could breathe deeply of the fresh air. He had good, satisfying work to do in tending the garden – without weeds or thistles to make it frustrating. If you live in the middle of a busy, noisy, dirty city, with a job that is continually frustrating, perhaps Adam's early days sound like a dream life.

But it was not good.

This sounds the first note in a minor key after the constant refrain of Genesis 1, 'And it was good . . . And it was good . . . And it was good.' Everything God made was good, but it was not good for the man to be alone.

In March 2020, Boris Johnson announced the first national lockdown in response to the Covid pandemic. Initially we were told it would be reconsidered after just three weeks. In fact, it was months before the restrictions were eased. During the lockdown, many of us experienced aloneness in a way that we had never done before.

I live on my own, so for nearly three months I had no physical contact with any other human beings at all. I do live very near to my family, so I was able to see my parents when I dropped their shopping off, and my brother's family over the garden fence. I still went out to do my weekly shop. And, of course, I was able to maintain contact with friends and work colleagues over the internet.

But by mid-June, despite my strongly introvert side having rather enjoyed the limited social interaction over the previous months, it was suddenly not OK. It was not OK to keep living in that kind of isolation. It was not OK that I couldn't give someone a hug. It was not OK that I couldn't sit in the same room as my friends and chat over a cup of tea. I was alone and it was not good.

Adam's aloneness was far greater than mine. He did not have family nearby – he did not have family at all. He didn't have friends he could phone or Zoom – he did not have friends at all. He did not have a church family he could interact with each week as we found ways to have some kind of shared experience of worship. He didn't have work colleagues, or checkout staff in the supermarket, or a postman who would smile and say good morning as he left parcels on the doorstep. He was completely alone.

A week or so after I first felt that deep sense of aloneness, the government in the UK announced their 'support bubble' scheme. If you were the only adult in your household, you were now permitted to join with another household. You could be in the same spaces, you could eat together, you could touch. It was the first announcement to acknowledge that the lockdown was taking an emotional toll, not merely an economic one. It recognised the aloneness that some people were experiencing and offered a solution: other people.

It was the same solution that God found for Adam. Having considered all the animals carefully, it was clear that none of them would resolve his aloneness. None of them could offer the companionship and help he needed. None of them could be his family or his community. None of them could be his wife.

We need other people

But for Adam no suitable helper was found. So the LORD God caused the man to fall into a deep sleep; and while he was sleeping, he took one of the man's ribs and then closed up the place with flesh. Then the LORD God made a woman from the rib he had taken out of the man, and he brought her to the man.
(Genesis 2:20–2)

The problem for Adam wasn't simply that he was unmarried. His aloneness went far deeper than that. He had no helper. That is, he had no one to help with his work and no one with whom to enjoy his rest time. There was no one he could seek advice from and no one with whom he could discuss the things he was learning.

God solved this problem by creating the woman. Just as Adam had been created from the dust to make it clear that he was part of the same physical creation as everything else, so Eve was created from Adam to make it clear that she was part of the same humanity. She, unlike all the other animals, was a suitable helper for Adam. She was fit to work alongside him, to be his companion, his friend, his family, his household and his community. Of course, the two of them together were only the seeds of all this. One person can't fulfil all our needs for human relationship and interaction. But together, Adam and Eve had the potential to create a wider community.

When people are introduced in the Bible, especially in the Old Testament, very often we are told what tribe they belonged to or given part of their family tree. Those genealogies and tribal identities are a way of setting people in a context. Who is David? Well, he is the son of Jesse, the son of Obed, the son of Boaz and Ruth. If you live in the same area as your parents and grandparents did, you've probably been introduced in a similar way. To some people I am best introduced as 'Ivor's daughter' and to others I'm the granddaughter of the Leeses, who had the shop on the high street. Those connections are our way of placing people in the community to which they belong.

It was unthinkable to the ancient Israelites that a person should end up tribeless. In situations where someone might potentially be left without a family identity, there were clear rules about who should take them in. This is what is happening in the book of Ruth, where Naomi claims Boaz as her 'kinsman-redeemer'. Naomi's husband has died, along with both her sons. She has no household to which she belongs on her return to Israel, but she can claim membership through the family line. No one should be left out on their own.

We live in a very different sort of society today, where it is easy for people to become isolated from their families and where loneliness is a huge problem. The aloneness of the pandemic lockdowns has ended for most of us, but long-term loneliness persists for far too many people, especially older people. According to research by Age UK, half a million older people do not see or speak to anyone on at least five or six days each week. Some 40% of older people say that the television is their main source of company.[1] This long-term loneliness is not good for anyone and it is not good for society. It can have a negative effect on both the physical and mental health of those who are lonely, but it also indicates a weakening of the network that makes up our communities. Ironically, the pandemic prompted something of a resurgence of community spirit as people volunteered to run errands and do shopping for those who couldn't leave their houses at all.

Being human means being made for relationship and community. It wasn't good for Adam to be alone and it's not good for any of us to be alone.

This is the wisdom of the author of Ecclesiastes:

Two are better than one,
    because they have a good return for their labour:
if either of them falls down,
    one can help the other up.
But pity anyone who falls
    and has no one to help them up.
Also, if two lie down together, they will keep warm.
    But how can one keep warm alone?
Though one may be overpowered,
    two can defend themselves.
A cord of three strands is not quickly broken.
(Ecclesiastes 4:9–12)

---

1 Based on research by Age UK and cited at: <www.campaigntoendloneliness.org/the-facts-on-loneliness/> (accessed 10 February 2023).

When I was at school, we were allowed to walk into the town in groups of three because, as it was explained to us, you needed one to have the accident, one to stay with them and one to go and get help. That's the point here: if you're on your own and something goes wrong, there's very little you can do about it. Another person in the situation transforms everything. A companion can help you out of trouble. A companion can keep you going. A companion can help to protect you. Working together can be more productive than each working separately.

What is true literally here in Ecclesiastes is also true metaphorically in a huge variety of situations. In many cases it doesn't even matter whether that person is a family member, a friend or an acquaintance. If your car has broken down and your phone is out of battery, a complete stranger can be the one to help you by calling the breakdown services. If a Twitter mob is baying for your blood, a person you have never met can step in to point out that they've misunderstood and should leave you alone. There are times when we all need the kindness of strangers.

Sometimes, of course, we need people who know us better than that, or who understand the difficult circumstances we're in. We need work colleagues who can see when we're not quite coping and will step in to shoulder some of the burden. We need friends who have known us for years and can point out where we're struggling to see our own mistakes. We need family members who will love us and care for us, no matter what. We need a whole network of people we can reach out to at different times. If you only have one person, aloneness is always lurking just around the corner. A healthy life is lived in relationship with many other people, in community.

Perfume and incense bring joy to the heart,
    and the pleasantness of a friend
    springs from their heartfelt advice.
(Proverbs 27:9)

As iron sharpens iron,
    so one person sharpens another.
(Proverbs 27:17)

For some people, the need for relationship and connection with others is obvious and instinctive. For others, it has to be learned and worked at. But no matter how much of an introvert you are by temperament, you still need other people in your life. Books may be easy, undemanding companions, but they are no substitute for people who can challenge us and comfort us, love us and lead us into new and better ways. We need the heartfelt advice of trusted friends, and the challenge of those who will sharpen our understanding and our behaviour. We cannot see our own blind spots; we need the help of others.

God has not designed us to be independent and self-sufficient. People are not supposed to act as separate units, working only for themselves. We're designed to need one another, to depend on one another. Like a colony of ants all busily doing their part, together we are stronger, healthier, better.

Throughout the Bible, we can see that God is interested in building a society, a community – not merely a group of separate individuals. God's people are a family. In the Old Testament, this is more or less a literal family, of all those descended from Abraham and thus related by blood, but in the New Testament it's made clear that family membership depends on faith more than blood.

When God saves a person, he saves them to become part of his people. God's people are a building, stones laid upon stones, so that together we become something much greater than a pile of rubble. God's people are a body, each part necessary for the whole to work as it was intended to.

Other people need us

Later on in the pandemic, I was part of a delightful support bubble with some dear friends who live about forty minutes from my house. Every week I would drive down on a Friday and spend the weekend in their warm, welcoming, chaotic house. It was wonderful. After a few weeks of this, I was surprised to be given a gift of a lovely candle. Surely they were the ones doing me the favour, and if anyone should be giving gifts, it was me?! But my friend replied, 'You have no idea how much difference it makes having you here.' They weren't alone in the same way I had been, but they were still feeling the cabin fever of all being cooped up together. I needed them, but wonderfully, it turned out that they also needed me.

The eye cannot say to the hand, 'I don't need you!' And the head cannot say to the feet, 'I don't need you!' On the contrary, those parts of the body that seem to be weaker are indispensable, and the parts that we think are less honourable we treat with special honour. And the parts that are unpresentable are treated with special modesty, while our presentable parts need no special treatment. But God has put the body together,

giving greater honour to the parts that lacked it, so that there should be no division in the body, but that its parts should have equal concern for each other. If one part suffers, every part suffers with it; if one part is honoured, every part rejoices with it.
(1 Corinthians 12:21–6)

In this section of 1 Corinthians, Paul is talking to the Church, the community of God's people, about the different gifts they each have and their interdependence. He uses the metaphor of the body to help them see how each one is needed, and that it is their difference which makes them so valuable. A body made up only of eyes or feet would be no use at all! The eye needs the hand to do what it sees needs doing. The head needs the feet to go to the place it wants. It is the same with the Church: we need the visionary leaders and the practical helpers. We need the people who pray, the people who preach and the people who put the chairs out.

Perhaps you look around at your church, your family, your local community and think that no one would notice if you weren't there. Perhaps you sometimes feel as though you don't have anything to offer. Maybe it seems as though no one needs you. But what is true of the church family is true of every community God puts us in: other people need you!

You are not replaceable, because you are unique. God made you and he placed you in the world where he wanted you to be. He has set you in a family and in a community, not only because he knows you need them, but because he knows they need you. You make a difference simply by being there. You make a difference because you bring your unique set of experiences, your unique personality, your unique abilities. And the more you build those friendships, the more strongly you will become embedded in the network and the more impact you will have.

Too often we think of relationships in transactional terms: what we can get out of them in exchange for what we put into them. But friendships are not business deals. Families are not companies. Communities are not factories. We can't measure the value we add to someone's life just by smiling and greeting them when we pass them on the street. We can't know how important a phone call or casual chat over the garden fence is in changing the way someone feels that day.

Sometimes I talk to women with very young children who find it extremely hard to get to church every week and feel as though it's hardly worth bothering, since they spend the whole service feeding, changing and keeping the baby from crying too much. But it is a huge encouragement to me and to the rest of the church to see them there and to know that they have made such a great effort to come and be with us. They may not be able to serve the church in any concrete ways, but their presence is a blessing to us all. The same is true of every person who simply turns up. We are all a blessing to one another.

After several months of being unable to meet together physically as a church in 2020, our first service of the pandemic took place outside. We weren't allowed to sit too close together, we couldn't sing together or share communion, we still wore face masks, along with our coats and gloves. The restrictions would have been unthinkable a year before, and yet it was the most joyous celebration. There was a party atmosphere as we gathered out on the grass. Young and old, families and single people, even a few dogs on their leads – we were together. And after those months of being kept apart, we knew more than ever how much every person there was precious. Every person there mattered. We needed all of them.

God did not make us to live in isolation as independent individuals. You need other people, and other people need you.

Questions to consider

1　Why does God create human beings to live in families and communities?
2　Look at Proverbs 27:6–10. What are the benefits of true friendships? How could you cultivate more of this kind of relationship in your life?
3　Are you someone who thrives in the company of others, or someone who finds that exhausting? What are the opportunities and dangers this gives you?
4　Why does the Church need all of its different members? Think of some concrete examples from your own local church – making sure to include yourself.

7

Being human means being sexual

The man said,

'This is now bone of my bones
  and flesh of my flesh;
she shall be called "woman",
  for she was taken out of man.'

That is why a man leaves his father and mother and is united to his wife, and they become one flesh. Adam and his wife were both naked, and they felt no shame. (Genesis 2:23–5)

From the beginning, the woman is one flesh with the man, because she is created out of his flesh. For this reason, we're told, women and men will become one flesh again, through the physical union of sex. Following the model established with Adam and Eve, all people are created as sexed beings; that is to say, as male or female. In this passage from Genesis 2, we also learn that women and men are sexual beings, created with the capacity and desire to be reunited in the flesh. As children go through puberty, they normally become conscious that they are sexual beings, with the capacity and desire for the one-flesh union of sexual intercourse.

The writer of Genesis is at pains to make us understand that sex is a good part of God's good creation. The nakedness of Adam and Eve was not accompanied by any shame, and in their sinless existence it did not need to be. There was nothing to be ashamed of and nothing to be embarrassed about. They could enjoy all the goodness of God's creation, including the delight they found in sex with each other.

What was true for Adam and Eve continues to be true: sex continues to be good! That is the point of Genesis 2:24, which draws a direct link from the shame-free union of Adam and Eve to the sexual union of every husband and wife. As a new family unit is formed, by a man leaving his parents' household, the new unit is secured by the physical joining of the man and the woman in sex.

If only that were all we needed to say on the matter. Sadly, as we all know, throughout human history the misuse of sex and sexuality has proved itself to be a source of shame and sin, and a cause for violence and despair. It has brought down empires and ended many apparently fruitful ministries. Sex has been the driving force in many people's lives, while for others it has been a private repository of shame and grief. Sex is powerful, therefore it can be dangerous. God's good gift of sex can have devastating consequences in the hands of sinners.

The secular world appears to be in thrall to sex. Sex permeates popular culture in music and films, on TV and in advertising. Sex education begins in primary schools and sexual experimentation is openly tolerated throughout secondary school life. There seems to be an expectation that everyone will be having sex as often as they choose, with whomever they choose, in whatever way they choose. The idea that an adult might be a virgin is often ridiculed, even if in reality levels of sexual activity may actually be declining.[1] Of course, even if other kinds of sexual activity are declining, the use of pornography by the majority of the adult population[2] ensures that sex is never far from people's thoughts.

If sex is the most important thing in our culture, and for many people the most important thing in their lives, then there is plenty we need to say about why God made us sexual people.

Sex is not necessary

The first thing we need to say is that, despite the overwhelming message of modern culture and media, sex is not actually necessary for a full, satisfying life. We've already seen in the previous chapter that Adam's problem was not specifically singleness, but aloneness. Singleness is not a negative choice in the Bible, and of course our model for perfect humanness, Christ himself, was single. He affirmed the pattern of marriage established in Genesis 2, but he chose not to take that path for himself. He lived an unmarried, celibate life, but he was still a sexual person, with normal capacity and desires. He *chose* to live an unmarried, celibate life.

Life is necessarily full of choices: we are limited and we can't do all things. That was true even for the Lord Jesus. He deliberately left the places where he was overwhelmed by

---

1 A survey of 2,000 adults in the USA found that 18- to 24-year-olds were less sexually active than adults in their later 20s to 40s: <www.auburnlane.com/is-gen-z-more-sexually-active/> (accessed 10 February 2023).
2 76% of UK men and 53% of UK women, according to a 2022 YouGov survey: <https://yougov.co.uk/topics/society/articles-reports/2022/07/01/how-often-do-britons-watch-porn> (accessed 10 February 2023).

demands for healing so that he could go elsewhere to preach the good news. He chose not to marry, we can assume, for similar reasons. His was an itinerant ministry. He did not have a home. He had a more important ministry than establishing a family and a household. But he was not alone. He had close friends and a wider circle of followers. He had a mother and brothers, an extended family, who continued to love and care for him. Being alone is not good for us, but the solution to that is not necessarily a sexual relationship.

> I would like you to be free from concern. An unmarried man is concerned about the Lord's affairs – how he can please the Lord. But a married man is concerned about the affairs of this world – how he can please his wife – and his interests are divided. An unmarried woman or virgin is concerned about the Lord's affairs: her aim is to be devoted to the Lord in both body and spirit. But a married woman is concerned about the affairs of this world – how she can please her husband. I am saying this for your own good, not to restrict you, but that you may live in a right way in undivided devotion to the Lord.
> (1 Corinthians 7:32–5)

In this passage from 1 Corinthians, Paul is discussing the questions of whether Christians should remain married and whether they should get married. Essentially, he is saying stay as you are. If you are married, don't leave; if you are engaged, honour that commitment; if you're not married, don't look for a spouse. But even then he makes exceptions: if you aren't married but find yourself burning with lust, then it's better to get married if you can. He realises that most people will want to get married and he is careful to say that there is nothing wrong with that. And yet, however much he hedges around it, Paul thinks it is better for Christians not to marry, so that they can give their full attention to serving the Lord.

This is an incredibly counter-cultural thing to say to anyone today. If a person chooses not to marry for their own reasons, we may accept it, though perhaps not quite understand it. If someone is single simply because they've never met the right person, we feel sympathy for them. But the idea that someone might choose not to marry in order to give themselves more fully to serving Christ seems unthinkable to many people, even to some Christians.

That's the choice I made, more than twenty years ago, and I am still convinced that it has been the right choice for me. It won't be the right choice for everyone, and probably not for most people, but it is a choice that we should help people to consider. There are many ways in which being single can increase our capacity for service, perhaps especially for women. And although it will mean choosing not to experience some great blessings, it does not mean choosing an unsatisfying, unfulfilling life. It does not mean choosing loneliness or aloneness. It does not mean giving up Christ's invitation to have life to the full.

Nor does it mean giving up our part in the great divine metaphor of salvation that is illustrated in marriage. The Christian life now is one of frustration, as we long and watch and wait for the return of the bridegroom. That is to say, it is the life of the single person, wondering how much more they can take, wondering if and when they will experience the delight and joy of married life. As single people, we know our bridegroom is coming, and we are not tempted to place our hopes in a human relationship that will always bring disappointment.

We are sexual people, but we do not need to be sexually active to live fully human lives.

Sinful sex

Sex is a good part of God's good creation, but like everything else in creation, our experience of sex has been twisted and broken by the effects of sin. The curse that God pronounces on Eve hints at this:

'I will make your pains in childbearing very severe;
    with painful labour you will give birth to children.
Your desire will be for your husband,
    and he will rule over you.'
(Genesis 3:16)

She will experience pain in childbearing, and as any woman can tell you, every part of our biological system connected with childbearing is painful: menstruation, infertility, pregnancy, labour and menopause. It should be no surprise that sex itself can be part of this sequence of painful processes. The second part of the curse indicates that there will be emotional and relational consequences of the fall, and these too will have an impact on sex.

Sex can be painful in a variety of ways. Sexual abuse and sexual assault are the most horrific ways to attack a person, having serious physical and emotional repercussions for the victim. Even within a consensual relationship, sex can be difficult and painful, as it involves becoming so vulnerable to another person. There may be issues of sexual dysfunction or sexual trauma. There can be powerful feelings of shame associated with sex or nakedness. And there is no guarantee that your partner will have the patience and understanding to help overcome such issues in order for the relationship to strengthen and flourish. Sex may become a battleground or a crying field as two sinners join together, each carrying a heavy weight of baggage.

Sex is not always the gift to be delighted in that it was for Adam and Eve before sin entered the world. Sometimes the loving thing to do is not to have sex. Always the right thing to do will be to show patience and kindness, gentleness, faithfulness and self-control. I can't give you any tips on how to have great sex by trying different positions or techniques. But I can tell you that the fullest expression of your sexuality is to be as godly as possible in the way you demonstrate your love for each other: to be self-giving not self-seeking.

Since the fall, it is not only sexual activity, but sexual desires that have been corrupted. We do wrong things *and* we desire wrong things:

> Because of this, God gave them over to shameful lusts. Even their women exchanged natural sexual relations for unnatural ones. In the same way the men also abandoned natural relations with women and were inflamed with lust for one another. Men committed shameful acts with other men, and received in themselves the due penalty for their error.
> (Romans 1:26–7)

The Bible makes it clear that sexual desire for a person of the same sex was not part of God's good creation. In Romans 1, Paul explains that it is a result of God's judgement on sinful society. It is easy to see how our contemporary secular society has exchanged the truth of God for all kinds of lies. It is easy to see how people worship their own created idols of wealth, fame or beauty. We should not be surprised to see the evidence of God's response to this in the sexual proclivities of men and women today.

In 2021, the UK census collected information about sexual orientation for the first time.[3] About 3% of the adult population ticked to indicate a non-heterosexual orientation,[4] 7.5% didn't answer and just under 90% indicated that they were heterosexual. That correlates to about one and a half million people in this country who have some form of sexual attraction to people of their own sex.

Remember that in Romans 1, Paul is talking about a whole society having abandoned God. The fact that some people in our culture experience same-sex attraction is simply an indication that we live in a society that has largely abandoned God. It is what we should expect in a largely atheist, secular culture like the UK. And because it is a judgement on society as a whole, we should certainly expect there to be people in our churches who are same-sex attracted, just as there are in the rest of society.

Sexual orientation is not, according to Paul, a punishment for personal, individual sin. It is a sign that we live in a sinful world. Like disability and disease, homosexual attraction

---

3 See: <www.ons.gov.uk/peoplepopulationandcommunity/culturalidentity/sexuality/bulletins/sexualorientationenglandandwales/census2021> (accessed 10 February 2023).
4 Options included 'gay or lesbian', 'bisexual' or 'other sexual orientation'.

exists because the whole creation has been distorted as a result of human sinfulness. We know that there was no blindness in the garden of Eden, but when Jesus is challenged about whose sin led to the blindness of a man in John 9, he is clear: it was not the man's fault, nor even his parents' fault. He was blind because we live in a broken world. In a similar way, the presence of same-sex attraction is not the result of any person's individual sin. It exists because we live in a broken world.

If you're a Christian who experiences same-sex attraction now, you can take comfort that one day God will deal with all the sexual temptations faced by human beings. Sexual orientation describes a particular form of temptation, not a sin. The penalty Paul talks about in Romans 1 is not for sexual orientation, but for shameful lusts and harmful acts. Many people who experience same-sex attraction live faithful, godly, celibate lives. They do not wallow in their lust, or let it lead them into ungodly sexual activity. God will honour them for their obedience and we must do everything we can to love and support them in this.

Of course, homosexuality is not the only way in which human sexual desires have been corrupted by sin. Within my lifetime social taboos around sex have fallen like dominoes: homosexual sex, kinky sex, polyamorous sex. As long as no one is being coerced or harmed, the argument goes, why should anyone care what turns you on?

Such things are not, in fact, a novelty. Leviticus 18 shows us that the Old Testament law included prohibitions on activities including incest, bestiality and child sacrifice. Presumably these needed to be outlawed because they were already known temptations within the Canaanite world. The beginning and ending verses of the chapter make it clear that such things were not merely forbidden to the Israelites for cultural or religious reasons. They were said to be detestable to the Lord.

The truth is that any kind of sexual activity outside of marriage is sinful. Adultery is sinful. Pre-marital sex is sinful. Sexual abuse is sinful. Pornography use is sinful.

Sexual sin is not more sinful than any other sin, but it can be more destructive and more deeply embedded. The beautiful, precious gift of sexual intimacy that God created for men and women is so easily broken and twisted by our sinful desires, it can be hard to remember how good sex is supposed to be.

God made us with the capacity and desire for one-flesh union with another person. It is normal to want to experience that and, alongside the physical pleasure, the emotional intimacy sex can bring. It can be hard to live without sex, even for people who have made a conscious choice to live a celibate life. How much harder it must be for people who would dearly love to be married, but have never had the opportunity. Harder still for those who only experience attraction to people of the same sex, and know that heterosexual marriage is unlikely ever to be possible for them.

Faithful Christian discipleship in this area can be incredibly costly. The temptations are everywhere, no matter what situation you are in. You may be married, struggling with the temptation to seek sexual gratification elsewhere. You may be single, unable to find a suitable Christian to marry, so you start looking outside the Church for sexual fulfilment. You may be attracted only to people of the same sex, and struggling to come to terms with a future without a partner. You may be turning to pornography on the internet and making sex into an act of self-gratification rather than self-giving. None of those temptations will lead to the satisfaction we are seeking. Sinful sex can never do what good sex does, which is to point beyond itself to the true satisfaction we will finally experience when our heavenly bridegroom returns to consummate our marriage.

There are so many ways in which our sex lives can be disappointing and frustrating. You may be a victim of abuse or assault, unable to overcome your traumatic response to intimacy. You may have medical problems, making it difficult or impossible to enjoy penetrative sex. You may bear guilt or shame from the way you have sinned in this area in the past. The wonderful news is that the Lord Jesus came to redeem us in every area of our lives. He takes away our guilt and our shame. He restores us and makes us new again. Whatever frustrations continue now, know that one day you too will experience the full joy and satisfaction of consummation, when Christ comes to take us home.

Faithful living now, whether that is in a marriage or as a single person, is the nearest we can come to knowing the joy that is waiting for us then. Let us encourage each other in this, and build communities in which the blessings of family and friendship are experienced by everyone, no matter what their marital status may be. Let us hold to the power of the Holy Spirit in our lives, transforming and strengthening us, so that we can live as God's holy people, pure and blameless.

Discipleship in this area is hard for many of us and incredibly costly for some of us, but on that day we will all know that it was worth it.

Questions to consider

1 How does the Bible's view of sex differ from that of the secular culture we live in?
2 Why is sex a good thing? What blessings can it bring?
3 Why is sex so dangerous when it is misused?
4 How does your local church celebrate and support single people? How are those people a blessing to the church?
5 How does your local church support people who experience same-sex attraction? How might those people be a blessing to the church?

8

Being human now means being a sinner

There are moments that will for ever split history into the before and after: the invention of the printing press, the assassination of Archduke Franz Ferdinand, the destruction of the World Trade Center. The first such moment comes in Genesis 3. Before this, the creation was as good as God could make it, which is to say very good indeed. Adam and Eve, the first human beings, lived in harmony with the world, with each other and with their Maker.

Our experiences of humanity may not completely live up to the ideal that the first two chapters of Genesis give us, but we have seen what we were intended and designed to be. God made us in his image, male and female, body and soul, for work, for community and as sexual people. Those are all good aspects of God's good creation of humanity and we should be seeking to live accordingly.

But in Genesis 3, through the actions of the serpent and the choices of Adam and Eve themselves, everything changes. They are deceived and seek to deceive. They wilfully disobey. They disbelieve what God has told them. And as a result, they face death.

Their sin has affected and infected the whole of humanity, with just one exception: the new Adam, Jesus Christ. The sinful actions of Adam and Eve had consequences that affected them body and soul, which frustrated their work and twisted their relationships. We all still live with those consequences infecting every part of the world and every part of our lives.

We are all sinners.

We are deceived and deceiving

Now the snake was more crafty than any of the wild animals the Lord God had made. He said to the woman, 'Did God really say, "You must not eat from any tree in the garden"?'

The woman said to the snake, 'We may eat fruit from the trees in the garden, but God did say, "You must not eat fruit from the tree that is in the middle of the garden, and you must not touch it, or you will die."'

'You will not certainly die,' the snake said to the woman. 'For God knows that when you eat from it your eyes will be opened, and you will be like God, knowing good and evil.'

(Genesis 3:1–5)

The serpent's tactics are cunning and sneaky. He casts doubt on what God said to Adam: 'Did God *really* say . . . ?' He distorts what God actually did say, because in fact they were free to eat from every tree in the garden but one. But notice Eve's response. She corrects the serpent, 'We may eat fruit from the trees', and yet she also alters God's command, adding in a section about touching the fruit. Finally, the serpent denies outright what God said, 'You will not certainly die.'

This first sin is all in the mind. Long before Eve reaches out and plucks a fruit from the tree to eat she has sinned. In the first moment where her thoughts are swayed by the serpent to doubt and distort God's word, she has sinned. The devil, seen here in the guise of the serpent, is a deceiver, and our sinful nature is all too prone to believe his lies.

The devil's lies are subtle and seductive. He will tell us what we want to hear, what we want to believe. He will offer us all the world's riches and pleasures, and dismiss the notion that there might be dangerous consequences in listening to him. What are the lies the devil tells you? Have you noticed them? Are there persistent lies that you find all too easy to believe? Perhaps he tries to persuade you that your sin doesn't matter, or that God doesn't care. Maybe he pretends that certain actions aren't really sinful after all. However much we know the truth of God's word, we are all susceptible to the devil's deceitful strategies.

It's not only the devil who deceives, however. Eve is fully complicit in the deceit. She distorts God's word just as much as the devil does. She seems to be persuading herself that God's command is far more restrictive than it really is, perhaps to show how unreasonable God has been that they aren't even allowed to touch the fruit from the tree of knowledge.

Our sinful nature makes us self-deceivers. We lie to ourselves about the depths of our sinfulness. We pretend that our motives are good when we know they are not. We find ways of persuading ourselves that it's fine to do things we know we ought not. 'God did not really say that' and 'God did not really mean this' are easy excuses to let ourselves off the hook. We are slow to examine ourselves in order to confess our sin, and quick to pronounce ourselves forgiven.

Have you ever found yourself retelling an event to yourself – rehearsing it in your head, as if you were explaining it to another person? I have. Sometimes it's innocent enough, imagining how I would make it sound funnier or more dramatic. But sometimes the retelling subtly changes my role in the event, or my motivation, to make me come out better. It's a lie! It's a way I deceive myself, forgetting the truth of my actions behind the better story I can tell.

Eve deceives herself and then she deceives Adam. She gives him the fruit and he eats it. We don't know exactly how much Adam had witnessed of the conversation with the serpent. It seems clear later on in the chapter that he knew he was eating the fruit God had forbidden, but we don't know how Eve persuaded him to do so. At the very least she offered him the fruit, implicitly inviting him to join her as if it were completely fine.

Sin is deceitful and sin makes us into deceivers. One of the most devastating effects of our sin is that it makes us unable to trust ourselves. Sin has an impact on our thoughts, our feelings and our desires. We cannot always rely on our logic, our instincts or our emotions. Sometimes we may be right, but sometimes we will be wrong, and as sinners we are not well equipped to tell the difference. That is one reason why we need the Holy Spirit dwelling within us, to help us make right judgements.

We are disobedient

Eve's sin may have begun in the head, but it very quickly manifests itself in deliberate action. She takes the fruit and eats it, even though she knows full well that God has forbidden her and Adam from doing so. Only a moment previously she was claiming that God had even forbidden them from touching it!

Our internal sinful nature will always show itself in outward, wilful disobedience. At the heart of sin is thinking that we know best. We don't listen to God and we don't want to listen to God, because we want to do what we want. Sometimes we know that we don't know best, but we still won't listen to God, because we want to do what we know to be wrong or to leave good undone.

We are all stroppy toddlers at heart. Life would be so much better for us if we did what our heavenly Father told us to, but we are rebellious and resistant. We stick our fingers in our ears and screw our eyes shut and ignore him with all our might. We repeat the same disobedience time and time again, no matter how clearly we can see that it is harming us. We rush greedily for the pleasure of instant gratification, even when past experience tells us that it is going to make us sick.

We are sinners by nature and that means we all fall into sinful behaviour again and again and again.

We are disbelieving

The root cause of Eve and Adam's sin was simply that they did not believe God. When God told them not to eat from the tree of knowledge, it was not an arbitrary rule given simply to test their obedience. It was given because the consequence of eating that fruit would be death. God knew this and warned them of it. They knew what God had said, but they did not obey because they did not believe him that death would be the result of their actions. They did not believe that his instruction was given for their benefit. They did not trust that he had their best interests at heart.

In Deuteronomy 9:23 Moses says, 'But you rebelled against the command of the LORD your God. You did not trust him or obey him.' Our sin is fundamentally disbelief. This is what Moses had to explain to the rebellious Israelites in the desert. Their rebellion (in this instance, building a golden calf to worship) resulted from their lack of faith. They did not trust God, so they did not obey God.

In the same way, our sin is the result of our lack of faith in God. We sin because we do not believe God when he tells us the consequences of sin. We sin because we do not believe that his laws are given for our benefit. We sin because we do not trust him to know what is good for us. If we believed what he has told us, we would be terrified of judgement, but we would also long to live the blessed life that results from obedience. We would not listen to our own untrustworthy thoughts and desires; instead we would put our trust in what God has told us we should do.

Paul says in Ephesians 2:3, 'All of us also lived among [the disobedient] at one time, gratifying the cravings of our flesh and following its desires and thoughts.' Sinners are simply doing what they want. They gratify the sinful cravings of the flesh (remember that 'flesh' means 'sinful nature', not 'body') and they follow its desires. Sinners are not, by nature, seeking a way out of their sinful, disbelieving state. Paul knows that sinful people are capable of doing wonderful things and even of wanting to improve themselves. But sinners will never, of their own accord, seek God. They will never undo their own unbelief.

We disbelieve because we are sinners and we are sinners because we do not believe. We are trapped in a devastating catch-22 situation, a vicious circle from which we are unable to escape. Worst of all, it is a vicious circle from which, by nature, we do not even want to escape. We are content to wallow in our sin and to revel in our rebellion.

Without the transforming, faith-giving work of the Spirit, which Paul goes on to describe in the next few verses of Ephesians, not only is there no way out, but there is nothing in us that would be looking for the exit.

We are cursed

We live in the aftermath. The sin of Eve and Adam splits all history into the paradise before and the realm of sin after. The transforming effects of sin are universal and devastating. God pronounces curses on the serpent, on Adam and on Eve, which have wide-ranging consequences for all humanity and all creation.

The curse on Adam has a consequence for the whole of creation. The ground itself is cursed because of Adam. It produces thistles and weeds to grow up and choke the good plants Adam is tending. Again, we can't usually draw a direct line between specific sins and their effect on creation. Nonetheless we can easily see how very broken the world has become. It is not hard to hear what Paul describes as creation's groans (Romans 8:22): earthquakes and hurricanes, tsunamis and volcanic eruptions, droughts and famines, pests and diseases that destroy crops. Tools break, food decays, dust piles up. The world has become a place where life is hard work. It is as if the rest of creation is working against us.

The curse on Eve has a direct impact on her physical body. There will be pain in childbearing for her and for all women after her. For all of us, specific sins may have physical consequences: some of our sins harm our own bodies; some sins harm other people's bodies. But we must be careful not to draw a direct line between an individual's physical suffering and their sin. We saw earlier that Jesus makes this point very clearly in John 9:2–3, when the Pharisees ask him whose sin has caused a man to be blind. Jesus tells them that the man was not blind as a result of his own sin or even his parents' sin. He was blind because blindness is part of our fallen world. Disability and disease are not natural to humanity. They are part of the broken world in which we live and a consequence of sin entering the world. But they are not given by God as punishment for specific sins. In God's good creation in Genesis 1 and 2 there is no sickness and no suffering, and neither will there be in the glorious renewed creation for all eternity.

As we've already seen, the curse on Eve also has an impact on human relationships. That she desires her husband doesn't sound like a bad thing, but the two parts of this curse must be read together: 'Your desire will be for your husband, and he will rule over you' (Genesis 3:16). Her desire will be such that it allows her husband to control her. This is not a healthy relationship. It speaks of manipulation and power-play.

And the effect of sin on human relationships is not limited to marriages or romantic relationships. In any human interaction, everyone involved is a sinner. Everyone involved tends to think they know best. Everyone involved tends to seek their own best interests at the expense of others. Even where there is true self-giving love, there can be miscommunication, conflict of interests and poor decision-making causing harm. Even when we can't identify specific sins as the cause of problems in a relationship, we should expect the effects of the curse to make things difficult and cause frustrations.

We are dead

And the LORD God said, 'The man has now become like one of us, knowing good and evil. He must not be allowed to reach out his hand and take also from the tree of life and eat, and live for ever.' So the LORD God banished him from the Garden of Eden to work the ground from which he had been taken.
(Genesis 3:22–3)

The consequence of eating the fruit of the tree of knowledge was death. The devil cast doubt on this and by the end of Genesis 3 we might be tempted to think that he was right. Adam and Eve are not dead.

They do not die instantly, because of God's patient mercy and kindness. God prevents them from immediately eating the fruit of the tree of life, which would condemn them to a cursed eternity. Instead, they are banished from the garden and thus banished from God's presence. They are cut off from God, the source of light and life. They are dead in their sins, unable to recover their sinless lives, helpless to escape the curses upon them.

Sin has changed everything. Sin is not core to humanity in God's good creation, but with the exception of Christ it is the universal human experience. We are all sinners: deceived and deceiving, disobedient, cursed in ourselves and living in a cursed world, and dead in our transgressions and sins. We cannot understand humanity without reckoning with our sin – in our hearts and minds, in our words and actions. Every part of who we are is distorted by sin and its consequences: the way we think, how we feel, the functioning of our bodies, our relationships with other people, our interaction with the rest of creation, and our life in the Lord.

In Adam, we are all sinners. Thank God that although we are all in Adam, he sent for us a second Adam, who was neither deceiving nor deceived, who was not disobedient or disbelieving, and who, though he died, rose again to new life. Praise God that in Christ we too may be freed from the power and penalty of sin, and rise again in him to new life. Praise God that our humanity is restored and renewed through Christ's work of salvation, as we shall see through the final chapters of this book.

Questions to consider

1 Read Genesis 3:1–5 again and note the different tactics the serpent employs. How is Eve complicit in this deceit?
2 In what ways do you notice the devil tempting you? Are you sometimes complicit in this by deceiving yourself?
3 How is faith (or lack of it) connected to sin?
4 What must sinners do to be saved? Why is this the only way?
5 Think about the main news stories today. What do they show us about human sinful nature?

9

Being human means being mortal

It is a truism universally quoted by preachers that only two things are certain in life: death and taxes. We all know that we are going to die one day. And yet many people manage to live in emotional denial of this universal truth. At least, many people in modern, wealthy societies do. Death for us happens largely behind closed doors, in clinical environments, carefully managed. Funerals are being reinvented as 'celebrations of life' rather than times of mourning and grief.

Despite this, death persists. I don't suppose many of us will forget 2020, but for me it has a particular resonance. Throughout that year I lost nine friends, family members or church family members. Some were elderly or terminally ill; others young, fit and healthy. Some died with Covid, but none died of Covid. A cycling accident, sudden heart attacks and the gradual creep of cancer all took their toll. I remember a time when I was afraid to turn on my phone every morning in case someone else had died.

During this time, of course, we were living through the first wave of the pandemic. News bulletins included daily death tolls. We watched footage from hospitals overwhelmed by patients they could not help. Many of those who died did so alone, separated from their loved ones. Many who grieved did so alone. The image of the Queen, alone in her pew at the funeral of her beloved husband, resonated powerfully with many who had suffered similar experiences.

We could no longer pretend that we were shielded from death. It became real in our society, perhaps for the first time in a generation, and it was frightening.

Death is not natural

In God's good creation, there was no death, only life. Death entered the world as a consequence of sin – both the spiritual death that is separation from God and physical death in which body is separated from soul. Death is not right or good. It is not the way things are meant to be.

When we hear about someone dying young, or someone killed in a tragic accident, we feel this very strongly. We imagine what their lives might have been, we think of all the joy they might have brought and the good they might have done. Death is not always the direct result of a specific sin, but it is a consequence of living in a world broken and twisted by sin; a world full of diseases and natural disasters, of careless accidents and unforeseen consequences.

That instinctive reaction against death is a lingering trace of paradise inside us, harking back to our origins in the garden where there was no death. Death is not what we were created for. That's why the penalty for murder and manslaughter is so severe in the Old Testament: to destroy life is the opposite of the creation mandate to be fruitful and multiply. It is a denial of creation and a wholesale adoption of the devil's goal of destruction. We are created for life, not death.

Our modern tragedy is that while certain kinds of death are rightly opposed, others are both permitted and encouraged.

In Chapter 2 we considered the problems of abortion and assisted suicide. The death of these people at the very beginning of their lives, before birth, or of people who may be near the end of their lives, or who are living with chronic illness or disability, is not thought to be wrong. Heidi Crowter, a campaigner who has Down syndrome, has fought hard for a change in the law, which currently permits the abortion of babies with Down syndrome and other disabilities up to nine months. The disabilities for which this is permitted can be as minor as a cleft palate, a condition easily treated after birth. Heidi's argument is that this law is discrimination: disabled babies are not protected in the way that able-bodied babies at this stage are. Their death is thought by some to be a blessing rather than a tragedy. Indeed, in Iceland and Denmark almost every baby with Down syndrome is aborted.[1] What ought to be a source of deep shame is seen as a medical achievement. It is grotesque and it is wicked.

I recently sat with a friend who cried as she grieved for the child she had lost in an early miscarriage. That death was no one's fault, and yet the wrongness of it was profoundly obvious. Death, whenever and however it comes, is wrong and unnatural, and everything in us should rage against it.

Grief is normal

'Grief is the price we pay for love.' After the tragic events of 9/11, these were the words spoken by our late Queen in

---

1 'In Denmark, the Danish Cytogenetic Central Register shows an average of 98% of babies diagnosed with Down syndrome before birth are aborted each year ... According to official statistics reported in the Icelandic Parliament in the period from 2008–2012, all babies diagnosed with Down Syndrome in Iceland were aborted': <https://thelifeinstitute.net/info/down-syndrome-and-abortion-the-facts> (accessed 10 February 2023).

her message of condolence to the families of those who had lost their loved ones. As the nation mourned her death in September 2022, many of us remembered these words in our own grief for our beloved sovereign. When a beloved friend or family member dies, we grieve.

It is not wrong to grieve, even for those we know to be safe in the care of the Lord. Even when death brings relief from long and painful suffering, it is not wrong for us to mourn. Death is never good. It is always a reminder of the brokenness of our world and the consequences of our sin. It is always a sign that things are not as they are supposed to be. Death separates us from our loved ones and that loss should, of course, make us sad. Grief is the price we pay for love.

Even the Lord Jesus himself grieved when his dear friend Lazarus died. 'Jesus wept. Then the Jews said, "See how he loved him!"' (John 11:35–6). Jesus wept in sympathy with Lazarus's sister and the others who were grieving. And he wept because of his own love for Lazarus. His grief was real, even though he surely knew the miracle he was about to perform. He grieved because of the wrongness of death, because of the separation from his friend, because of this clear evidence of the brokenness of the world. If even Jesus wept, we should not be ashamed of our own grief.

People need to grieve. One experience of the pandemic I hope never to repeat was attending funerals online, while sitting at home alone. Paul tells us that we should 'mourn with those who mourn' (Romans 12:15) as part of our expression of Christian love. We need to support our brothers and sisters in their grief. We can always grieve because of the wrongness of death and the brokenness of the world, and sympathise with those who have been separated from loved ones. We can always sit with someone as they cry, we can give hugs and make tea, we can hold their hand and remind them that they are not alone. We can give them permission to rage against death and be bitterly sad.

We need funerals. We need times of mourning. Perhaps there is also space for a memorial service or thanksgiving for a person's life later, but we shouldn't be rushing past the initial stages of grief. No matter how prepared you think you may be, no matter how much you know it is coming, or even wish for it as blessed relief from suffering, death is always shocking. It is always stark in its reality. It is final and fierce, and we should not paper over it with platitudes.

People who die do not become stars shining in the night sky. Nor have they merely gone into the next room. They do not continue living 'in your heart', or become your guardian angel. Whatever soothing suggestion well-meaning friends might use to help us feel less sad cannot change the reality of death. False comfort is, in the end, no comfort at all.

When a believer dies, there is true comfort in knowing they are safe with Christ and in knowing we will one day be reunited with them in the new creation. This hope doesn't mean that there is no place for Christian grief, but that we 'do not grieve like the rest of mankind, who have no hope' (1 Thessalonians 4:13). Christians grieve, as Christ grieved, but not without hope.

When an unbeliever dies, our only comfort lies in knowing that God is both good and just, and that we can entrust our loved one to him. We may have no confidence in their salvation, but nor can we know with any certainty that they continued in rebellion against the Lord to their last breath. If the thief on the cross could be saved, as we know he was, we know that the possibility of repentance and faith continues to the very final moment of a person's life.

We are all mortal

Every death is a reminder that all of us are mortal, that death is coming for us all. There is no escape route, no fire exit. Although we talk frequently about 'saving lives', the truth is that the very best medical care in the world can only prolong life, not save it.

Our mortality is the harshest reminder of our limitations. We do not know the number of days left to us, but we know it is a finite number. For some, this awareness of mortality is a motivation to squeeze as much adrenaline-fuelled excitement as possible into every day: climbing mountains, visiting extraordinary places, jumping out of planes and into volcanoes. For others, it is a source of despair and depression: what's the point of anything if we're all going to die anyway? Job expresses this viewpoint with anguished insight:

My days are swifter than a weaver's shuttle,
    and they come to an end without hope.
Remember, O God, that my life is but a breath;
    my eyes will never see happiness again.
(Job 7:6–7)

Life is short and swift, and it is easy to see how this awareness can lead to melancholy at the pointlessness of it all. Without Christ we are indeed without hope. Why not wring every last drop of instant gratification out of the few short days we have? Or why even bother to try? What does it matter?

Not everyone falls into one or other of these two traps. Many people find purpose in this life by helping others, by making contributions to the wider good of humanity, by raising the next generation. But there is an underlying bleakness to human existence that is hard to combat without any sense of something bigger than ourselves.

That underlying bleakness is serious and real. Physical death matters so much because it is a reminder of spiritual death, which leads to eternal death.

> Then I saw a great white throne and him who was seated on it. The earth and the heavens fled from his presence, and there was no place for them. And I saw the dead, great and small, standing before the throne, and books were opened. Another book was opened, which is the book of life. The dead were judged according to what they had done as recorded in the books. The sea gave up the dead that were in it, and death and Hades gave up the dead that were in them, and each person was judged according to what they had done. Then death and Hades were thrown into the lake of fire. The lake of fire is the second death. Anyone whose name was not found written in the book of life was thrown into the lake of fire. (Revelation 20:11–15)

Physical death comes to us all and, after death, judgement. For those whose name is written in the book of life, there is life. For those whose name is not written in the book of life, there is the second death. The death of eternal destruction. The death of eternal punishment. The death of eternal separation from God. This death will be final and for ever. It is the death that Adam and Eve were warned about in Genesis 2:17. It is sure and certain, and the only escape from it is through God's mercy on those whose trust is in Christ.

Christ has the victory

When the perishable has been clothed with the imperishable, and the mortal with immortality, then the
saying that is written will come true: 'Death has been
swallowed up in victory.'
(1 Corinthians 15:54–5)

Thanks be to God, indeed! In Christ we know that our faith is not only for this life; that death will not be our end. We who are perishable will be clothed with the imperishable and we who are mortal will be clothed with immortality.

Our time in this creation is still limited by death, but our lives have meaning and purpose far beyond that time. What we do here and now has eternal significance, for ourselves and for others. Our mortality is a reminder that we do not have to do everything. We are not responsible for completing the task. We put our trust in Christ who builds his Church and we live our lives in faithful discipleship doing the works he has prepared in advance for us to do. The promise of immortality is a promise that what we can do with our limited capacity has true value. We cannot do it all, but what we do is nevertheless significant. We are building God's everlasting kingdom. We are bearing witness to his everlasting glory. We are beautifying ourselves in preparation for our wedding day. We are working now so that one day we will enjoy an enduring rest. We live now in order to be ready for eternal life.

Questions to consider

1 Why do human beings die?

2 Read John 11:17–44, paying attention to the different ways people respond to Lazarus's death. Why does death prompt such different reactions?

3 Are you scared of dying? Does John 11 help to allay your fears?

4 How can Christians help people to face up to the reality of our human mortality? What hope and comfort can we offer?

10

Christ, the true human

In the TV series *Fake or Fortune*, Fiona Bruce and various experts in art history examine paintings to determine whether they are really the work of famous and important artists – or worthless fakes. It is a fascinating process involving cutting-edge science, historical investigation and the judgement of experts. Very often it is the last of these that is the crucial evidence in making the final decision. You or I might look at a painting and think it seems a bit like something Van Gogh might have produced, or Rembrandt or Leonardo da Vinci. But an expert who has spent all his life studying the real works of the artist can tell by instinct what is genuine and what is fake.

In this survey of the Bible's teaching about humanity, we've learned a lot from the way in which human beings were originally created as male and female, body and soul, for work and for relationship, in the image of God. We know that our experience of humanity is profoundly distorted by sin and its consequences, including death. But there is still one true human, one example of the Creator's work that shows us what we are meant to be. It is by studying Christ, the perfect example of humanity, that we learn what true humanity is.

Fully human in every way

. . . he had to be made like them, fully human in every way. (Hebrews 2:17)

This is the astonishing truth of the Incarnation, that the eternal Son of God, of one being with the Father, true God, had to be made like us, fully human in every way. The Creator of the universe, who upholds all things, became the baby who was laid in a manger at the first Christmas. How could his divine nature be encompassed within a human body? It is a mystery and a miracle.

He does not stop being God the Son. He does not give up his divine nature or his eternal being. But he takes on human nature. In his one person he has both divine nature and human nature. And as we have seen, human nature is to be both body and soul. In both body and soul, then, Christ became human.

When he took on that human nature, Christ submitted himself to human limitations of place and time. He was in one place at one time, rather than all times and all places. As he went through childhood he learned and grew (Luke 2:40). His body worked like ours: he needed food and became tired, he felt pain, he bled when he was whipped. His inner being, his soul or spirit, worked like ours: he thought, he felt, he wanted things. In the garden of Gethsemane, he submitted his will to that of the Father.

And as he died, his body was separated from his soul (Luke 23:46). His death was a human death. The eternal Son of God did not die according to his divine nature, but he did die a human death according to his human nature. His body was laid in the tomb, but his spirit was with the Father in paradise.

Just as Adam and Eve were created to work, so Christ followed this same pattern of work and rest. He worked with his hands as a carpenter, creating and problem-solving (Mark 6:3), and then he worked in his public ministry, so much so that he had to get up very early to find time to be alone and pray (Mark 1:35). He rested on the Sabbath, but he understood that Sabbath rest did not mean going hungry or leaving others to suffer (Mark 2:23 – 3:5). He did not live a life of idleness or leisure, but one of purpose, diligently working for the benefit of others.

It was not good for Adam to be alone. He needed a helper in his work, a wife to form his family unit and from which all community could follow. Christ, born into a family, never experienced the aloneness of Adam. His parents, especially his mother, and his brothers appear throughout the Gospel accounts. They loved him and were concerned for him, even when they did not understand him. Christ did not marry or have sex, but this did not make him less than fully human. He surrounded himself with fellow-workers and friends. The 'disciple whom Jesus loved' was surely not the only disciple Jesus loved. There were seventy followers, twelve apostles and an inner circle of Peter, James and John. He enjoyed the friendship of Mary, Martha and Lazarus. The women who attended his burial loved him. For all his uniqueness, Christ did not set himself apart from his community. He invested in human relationships, even when he knew those friends would betray him and disown him. He lived a human life.

The perfect image of God

Christ is in very nature God, and thus he is the perfect image of God, the exact representation of his being, as the author of Hebrews tells us (Hebrews 1:3). If we want to know what God is like, we must look to Christ. But it's also true that human beings are the image of God (Genesis 1:27), so if Christ is the perfect image of God, he is also the perfect human being. Which means that if we want to know what it means to be human, we should also look to Christ.

When a person makes a mistake, sometimes we'll remind them, 'You're only human', as a way of pointing out that we all make mistakes. Perhaps it is a good way of distinguishing humans from machines, although if you've ever been at the receiving end of a computer error you might think differently. In any case, our shortcomings do not make us more human. Rather it is the opposite: the more we become like Christ, the more we become like God, and therefore the more fully human we become, in the likeness of God.

In his earthly life, Christ demonstrates God's love, and thus how we should love. He embodies God's grace and mercy, and thus models how we should be gracious and merciful. He puts every characteristic of God's nature into practice, and thereby gives us the example we need of how to live godly human lives. There are so many aspects of Jesus' character we could examine here, since his whole life shows us how to live, but we will focus on three areas.

Serving, not being served

Whoever wants to become great among you must be your servant, and whoever wants to be first must be slave of all. For even the Son of Man did not come to be served, but to serve, and to give his life as a ransom for many. (Mark 10:43–5)

Jesus Christ, King of kings and Lord of lords, deserves all the honour and glory the world can bestow. And yet he did not come to lord it over his people, demanding the service that is his by right. He came to serve his people. He came to give himself for his people: his life as a ransom for ours. In this passage from Mark's Gospel, the disciples are quarrelling among themselves about who will have the places of honour at Christ's right and left hand. They are seeking glory – unlike Christ, who was willing to serve humbly. His service was for our benefit, but it is also our example to follow.

If we want to live out our true humanity, we will seek to be like Christ in this respect, preferring to serve others than to be served. We will have the mindset of Christ, looking not to our own interests but to those of others (Philippians 2:4). We will be generous with our money, hospitable in our homes, free with our time. We will not lord it over others, even when we are in a position of responsibility in the home, the workplace or at church. Our leadership will be like Christ's: true service.

You may be aware of some of the recent scandals of Christian leadership in the UK and elsewhere. Some of these scandals concern sexual sin, and others are about bullying and domineering behaviour. In every case, they involve abuse of power. It is a devastating indictment on the Church when its ministers abuse their positions like this. Ministers are, literally, servants: the Greek word *diakonos* (deacon) means both servant and minister. Pastors are, literally, shepherds – those who should protect their flock, even when it means laying down their lives (John 10:11).

Christians are not immune to the temptation of power. It can be a heady thing, discovering that people will listen when you speak, that they will do what you say. Many years ago, I was a schoolteacher. I found that it was all too easy to become a bully in that situation, precisely because it was part of my job to keep control, and exercise discipline in the classroom. I didn't like the person I was becoming in the face of that temptation, so I left. But it would have been easy to stay, and it would have been easy to pretend I was just doing what my job required. We are all self-deceivers, and the temptation to wield our authority to serve our own ends is very strong.

Christ shows us a better, truer way to live. Christ in his humanity and his humility shows us how to serve, not to be served.

Forgiving, yet without sin

Human beings are all sinners in need of forgiveness, yet we are often slow to forgive others. Christ, by contrast, was a human being without sin, but was nevertheless quick to forgive.

It is impossible for us to imagine even a single day, a single hour, without sin, let alone more than thirty years of life. Yet that is how Christ lived. He grew through the toddler years and the teen years without once giving in to the temptations we all face. He lived a celibate life, without lust and without treating women as objects for his use. He faced opposition and persecution, and was the victim of injustice and insult. But he did not sin. He was blameless in his fulfilment of the law, and his love of the Lord was complete. He never needed God's forgiveness, nor that of any other person.

He did not need forgiveness, but he offered forgiveness. Jesus forgave the sins of the paralysed man before he could even articulate his repentance (Mark 2:1–5). Jesus forgave the sinful woman who washed his feet in her tears, anointed him with perfume and wiped his feet with her hair (Luke 7:36–47). Most notably, while dying in agony on the cross, Jesus prayed for God's forgiveness of those who were crucifying him (Luke 23:34).

Jesus' life demonstrated God's forgiveness, and Jesus' death provided the grounds for God's forgiveness. Because he died, whoever believes in him shall not be condemned, but forgiven. Thus when we pray, Jesus tells us, we can say, 'Forgive us our sins as we forgive others.' We have grounds to ask for God's forgiveness because of Christ's death on the cross, which has paid the penalty for our sin and brought us into new life.

As we are forgiven, so too must we forgive others. If the sinless Christ can forgive us sinners, how much more should we sinners forgive those who have wronged us. Our forgive-ness is so strongly linked to our forgiven-ness that Jesus uses it as a test: 'For if you forgive other people when they sin against you, your heavenly Father will also forgive you. But if you do not forgive others their sins, your Father will not forgive your sins' (Matthew 6:14–15).

Forgiveness is not natural to our sinful nature, which likes to hold grudges and seek vengeance. Forgiveness is character-istic of God and only of human nature in so far as it is still bearing the image of God. Christ, perfectly in the image of God, is a forgiver. For us, if we are forgiven in Christ, we become those who are also able to forgive. If you are not a forgiver, you are not living up to your true humanity. Our 'forgiving-ness' should be a sign of our 'forgiven-ness'.

Gentle, but honest

When Jesus describes himself, he says he is 'gentle and humble in heart' (Matthew 11:29). Even when he is riding into Jeru-salem, surrounded by crowds who are cheering for him, he comes as a king who is gentle, riding on a donkey rather than a warrior's stallion (Matthew 21:5). Jesus' gentleness is evident throughout the Gospel accounts as he deals tenderly with those who are weak, vulnerable and outcast. He is welcoming to children, gentle with those who are sick, kind to those who are overlooked by others.

And yet there are times when Christ seems far from gentle. Immediately after his entry into Jerusalem, he proclaims judgement on the Pharisees and woe to Jerusalem. He overturns the tables of the market traders in the temple. He does not shy away from speaking hard truths to those who offer half-hearted discipleship (Matthew 8:18–22; Mark 8:34–8; 10:21–2) or to those who will face persecution in the future (Mark 13:9–13; John 15:18–21). This gentle king is also the judge of all mankind.

Jesus does not avoid subjects that might cause disagreement or controversy. He never offers false comfort or false hope. He does not shy away from rebuke or condemnation. He knows that following him is a hard road for his disciples and he does not make false promises about that. One of the ways in which Christ demonstrates his care for us is through the honesty he is willing to give us.

All too often, we find ourselves choosing between gentleness and honesty. We want to be kind and tender with people who are hurting and those who are weak, so we comfort them with meaningless words that do not address the reality of their situation. Or we know we must be bold and courageous in speaking the truth, so we ride roughshod over people's feelings and ignore their suffering.

Christ is a model for our human communication and our human relationships. In all things, including but not limited to our evangelism, we need to be both gentle and truthful. We need to care for people, to recognise their struggles and their weaknesses, to be patient and kind. But we know that we will only be able to offer real help and support if we are honest with them. They need to hear the true gospel, about the true Saviour, who rescues us from the reality of our sin and offers us true hope for eternity.

In every way, Jesus is a model for us. He is our example for enjoying the company of friends as much as he is for bearing suffering patiently. He shows us how to live without giving in to temptation and how to love others, even when they sin against us. He teaches us to pray and shows us how to prioritise prayer in a busy life. He celebrates with those who are celebrating and he mourns with those who mourn.

It is perhaps counter-intuitive, but I think it's true to say that those people we think of as the finest humans are those who are most godly in character. It is the people who serve humbly and tenderly, those who forgive fully and seek forgiveness swiftly, and those who speak the truth in love. This is how to be most human: be like Christ.

Questions to consider

1 Look at Hebrews 2:14–18. Why is it so important that Christ was fully human?

2 A number of years ago, it was common for Christians to wear wristbands with 'WWJD' on them, as a reminder to ask 'What Would Jesus Do?' in any situation. Do you think this is a useful question for Christians to ask themselves? Why or why not? Is there a better question to ask?

3 Which of the human characteristics of Christ discussed in this chapter do you find it hardest to follow? Spend some time looking at the Bible passages mentioned in that section, reflecting on how Jesus demonstrated this. Pray for his help.

11

Being redeemed

The history of slavery is shameful and horrific in all its forms. In creation, human beings were made to rule and subdue the earth, not to be ruled over and stripped of all autonomy. We were made to work, for the benefit of ourselves and others, but we were not designed for forced labour. To enslave a person is to deny the image of God in them. It is to treat them as if they were not human.

The fact that slavery is dehumanising is why it is such a powerful metaphor for humanity trapped in sin and death. Sin dehumanises us, entrapping us in a life that denies the image of God in us. It makes no difference that sin is a self-inflicted slavery; that it is our own sinful nature and desires keeping us enslaved. It is a slavery that strips us of our humanity.

In the ancient world, slaves who were able to amass enough money were permitted to purchase their own freedom. For most slaves, this was an unimaginable dream, since they had no opportunity to earn any money, or very little. Alternatively, someone else might pay the price on their behalf. In this way a slave could be redeemed. They could be freed from their enslavement and live accordingly.

Slaves to sin

In our sin, we are like those slaves who dreamed of being able to purchase their freedom, but in reality could never gather more than the odd coin, soon to be lost again. We could never build up enough credit to purchase our own freedom, for two reasons: God's standards are perfect and sin infects all our lives.

God's standards are perfect

In his judgement of our lives, the pass mark is not 50% but 100%. It is not enough to argue that there is more good than bad, when he demands that there be no wrong at all. This is not an arbitrary demand on God's part, or a malicious one, designed to make us all fail. God requires perfection, because he is perfect. God demands complete holiness, because he himself is holy. The Bible describes God's holiness as fierce and fiery. His holiness destroys sin. Sinners cannot stand in the presence of a holy God, because his holiness will simply destroy them. It does not matter how much good there is in us; if there is any sin, we will not survive.

Sin infects all our lives

This does not mean that we never do anything right, but that our sinful nature affects us in every way. Nothing we do is perfectly good, in thought and word and deed. There are always mixed motives, mixed feelings, imperfect actions. We cannot stop that impulse of jealousy or envy. We seek to impress other people with outward displays of generosity. We inwardly sneer at or judge or dismiss people we pretend to like.

As the psalmist says and Paul reiterates:

> There is no one righteous, not even one;
>   there is no one who understands;
>   there is no one who seeks God.

All have turned away,
    they have together become worthless;
there is no one who does good,
    not even one.
(Romans 3:11–12; cf. Psalm 14:2–3)

There is, then, no possibility of us redeeming ourselves. There is no way out of our slavery, and in some terrible cosmic version of Stockholm syndrome, the truth is that we do not even seek to be freed.

Since the first sins of Adam and Eve, all human beings have suffered under the curses pronounced by God. The consequences of these are seen in the natural world, in human relationships, in disease, disability and disasters. The whole creation groans under the curse. But for human beings the curse represents an even more serious problem: we are cursed by the Lord God to be banished from his presence. The curse of the law is not an impersonal status granted mechanistically through a legal process. The curse of the law is God's personal response to our sin, cutting us off from him.

Under the curse we are held captive. We cannot free ourselves from its bonds. We cannot force our way back into God's favour. We would not want to do so, even if it were somehow possible. We are trapped in a prison of our own making, by our own sinful nature, and we are powerless to save ourselves. Under the curse our humanness only twists further into decay and depravity.

Sin is like a cancer, spreading, forcing its way deeper and deeper into our bodies, taking away more and more of our normal human functions, until eventually the body shuts down. The more that sin infiltrates every part of our being, the less human we become. Without Christ there is no chemotherapy that can stop the cancer of our sin.

We need someone else to pay the price for our freedom. We need a redeemer.

Christ, our Redeemer

The Bible gives us a large-scale lived illustration of redemption in the history of the exodus. The whole of the Israelite people had ended up in slavery in Egypt. Pharaoh refused to let them go and they could not pay a price for their freedom. They needed a redeemer, but there was no one who could pay the price. The only redeemer who had the power to act in their situation was God. God stepped in, and set his people free. There *was* a price, though not a monetary one, nor a price paid to Pharaoh. The price was paid throughout the ten plagues, with their destructive effects on the river, the crops and the people of Egypt. Most devasting was the final plague: the death of the firstborn. The price of the Israelites' freedom was paid through the death of the Passover lambs.

God tells us very early on in the Bible what a human life is worth: a life must be paid for a life. That is why the price paid for the freedom of the enslaved Israelites entailed the death of a sacrificial lamb. That is why the price Christ paid for each one of us entailed his death. Christ gave himself for us. He gave his own life in order to redeem ours: '... our great God and Saviour, Jesus Christ, who gave himself for us to redeem us from all wickedness and to purify for himself a people that are his very own' (Titus 2:13–14).

Christ owed no price for his own freedom. Christ was not enslaved as a result of a sinful nature. He was fully human but entirely without sin. The price he paid, therefore, was not credited to his account but to ours. Because he was not merely human, but the fully divine Son, dying as a man, Christ's one life, freely given, was worth enough to pay for many billions of lives. He has paid enough to redeem every person who puts their trust in him to do so. We can be confident and secure in our redemption, because it is fully paid for by Christ. No more is needed and no more will be demanded. We are safe in our freedom.

There is another situation in the Bible that involves a redeemer. When a woman was left widowed and without sons, she could end up without a household to belong to and without the protection of a male relative. In such a case, she could apply to a male relative to be her kinsman-redeemer. As we have seen, this is what happened to Naomi in the book of Ruth. Boaz became her kinsman-redeemer, when the nearer male relative declined to take up his responsibility (Ruth 4:1–10).

This is not redemption from slavery, nor redemption from debt. This kind of redemption is about bringing people back into the family, who have been left outside. It is a helpful model for our redemption, because it reminds us that redemption is relational, not merely transactional. Christ's redemption of us brings us out of the banishment that Adam and Eve earned with their sin, and back into relationship with God. He brings us into God's household, God's family.

Being a redeemed human means being safe and secure in the family household of the Lord.

Redeemed for the Lord

You are not your own; you were bought at a price.
(1 Corinthians 6:19–20)

With the creation of Adam, God established all humanity. With the salvation won through Christ, God is establishing a new humanity, a new people for his very own. This new humanity is like the first in many respects: we are male and female, body and soul, made to work and to be in community. But this new humanity is not like the first, for it is not held captive to sin. It has been redeemed from the curse and set free to live in Christ. And because of that, we will be even more truly human as redeemed sinners in the new creation than Adam and Eve were in the garden before they sinned.

This new humanity is secure in a way that the first was not. In Adam, we were dependent on Adam's shaky ability to hold fast to obedience, and our own similarly doomed attempt. In Christ we can rely on Christ's sure and certain work of redemption, which has bought our freedom. It does not depend on us, but on him. He has redeemed us from wickedness and he is purifying us for himself, so that we will be a people of his very own. As Christ's redeemed humanity, we are secure in him, now and for the future. We need not be anxious about our own weakness and our ongoing sin, because our redemption does not depend on our efforts to secure it. We depend on Christ, whose work is complete and who does not change. We can trust him, even though we cannot trust ourselves.

This security does not depend on our feelings of assurance. It is a normal experience for Christians to go through times of doubting their salvation. After I became a Christian as a teenager, I think I prayed a prayer committing my life to the Lord approximately once a week for the first year. I wasn't sure I had done it right, or that I had really meant it, so I kept doing it just in case. Perhaps you have had more serious times of doubt because of persistent sin, or ongoing fears about the sincerity of your faith. In those times, the most helpful thing is to remember the objective fact of salvation: Christ died to pay the price for our sin. It doesn't depend on the quality of our faith but on the object of faith. That is, even if we have doubts and we feel that our faith is weak, our salvation is secure in Christ. His grip on us is strong, even when we are wavering and stumbling.

In this new humanity we are blessed, not cursed. In Galatians 3, Paul says that the blessing of Abraham comes to Gentiles through Christ's redemptive work (Galatians 3:26–9). This blessing on Abraham and his descendants signified that they were God's chosen people, the 'nation' that would show the world God's love and saving power. The blessing consisted of being fruitful and multiplying, of possessing a land to settle in, and of being a blessing throughout the world (Genesis 12:1–3). These blessings once belonged to Adam and the first humanity. Abraham and his descendants were to be the new start, blessed rather than cursed, but they too were sinners. We cannot be redeemed by Abraham – only by Christ. In Christ, however, we receive all the blessings that were once Adam's and all the blessings that were promised to Abraham (Galatians 3:7–9).

The new humanity that Christ has redeemed us for is Spirit-filled. God is working within us to purify us and empower us to live our new lives, as we'll be looking at more in the next chapter. The Spirit enables us to withstand the seductive charms of sin and to put our trust in God's good plans for our lives. The Spirit works in us to shape us into the likeness of Christ, the model of true humanity. As we grow in the Spirit, bearing his fruit in our lives, we embrace our new, true humanity as we were always intended to be, in the image of God.

It is a wonderful thing to be redeemed from the curse. It is good news indeed that we are held fast, secure in the redemption Christ has won for us. It is a glorious truth that we have the Spirit dwelling within us, remaking us into our new humanity. It is a marvellous blessing to receive all God's promises through Christ.

Questions to consider

1 Why do sinners need to be redeemed, not only forgiven?
2 What are the blessings that redemption brings for us?
3 Have you ever doubted your redemption? What grounds do we have for confidence in our salvation?
4 How is this new humanity 'in Adam' better than the first humanity 'in Christ'? How does it change our view of what it means to be truly human?

12

Being new in Christ

There's always one person at the gym who has a lean, toned, perfectly proportioned body that moves easily through a lengthy workout of weights and cardio. It's hard not to be impressed by their commitment and the results of their regime. But if you're anything like me, you'll find that their example doesn't help you to struggle through your ten minutes on the treadmill before reaching for a bar of chocolate. A perfect example is no use to those of us without the willpower to imitate it.

Christ gives us the perfect example of how to be human, but his example is not enough to help us overcome our sinful nature. He shows us how we ought to live, but in doing so his life serves as a reminder of how far short we fall.

Thankfully, Christ's life on earth is much more than a model for humanity that we're supposed to try to copy. Christ's life, his death and his resurrection are the means by which God achieves our salvation. Christ's death destroys death and Christ's life wins for us a new life. His resurrection is the birth of a new humanity, restored and renewed for the new creation. We are no longer condemned to be dead in Adam; we can be made alive in Christ.

New life by the Spirit

As Christians, we have probably become so used to the idea of being born again that we don't notice just how strange it is.

When Jesus tells Nicodemus that he must be born again (John 3:3), Nicodemus questions how such a thing could possibly happen. How can a person go back into his mother's womb?

But as we have seen, all of us who are descendants of Adam and Eve are born as heirs of sin and death. The humanity we inherit is infected by sin in every part, and our diagnosis is terminal. It's not possible to remove our sin surgically, nor to treat it with medication until we are healed. We are riddled with sin, body and soul, and there is no cure. We need to start all over again.

That is why God gives us new birth into a new life as part of a new humanity.

In this new life, this rebirth, we do not inherit Adam's sin but Christ's righteousness. In this new humanity we are not doomed to death; instead we have a living hope (1 Peter 1:3).

The vivid prophecy of Ezekiel 37 paints a picture of a valley full of skeletons. The people who were once there have been dead for so long that all their flesh has rotted away. Their dry bones are all that remain until God summons a wind to breathe new life into the remnants of these corpses. Just as God breathed life into the lifeless clay in order to make Adam live, so he breathes life into these dry bones in order to make them live. He puts flesh on the bones, and tendons on the muscles, and covers them with skin. He breathes life into them by his Spirit and they come to life.

What Ezekiel saw in this vision is the reality of what has happened in every Christian believer. We were those corpses whose flesh had rotted away, so dead were we in our sins (Ephesians 2:1). We needed God to breathe his Spirit into us, to give us new life in Christ. This new life we have in Christ is demonstrated in the new lives we lead.

New life in the power of the Spirit

Change is hard for most of us. Whether it's learning to adapt when a baby arrives in the family, or learning the ropes in a new job, it takes time for us to let go of old habits and build new ones. Remember the Israelites in the desert who had been brought out of the harshest slavery and oppression yet still looked back at their old lives fondly (Numbers 11:5)! There is comfort in familiarity, even when we know that we would be better off if we made changes.

The same is true when we are born again. We have a new life that is better by far, but the old life still exerts a pull on us. That's why Paul repeatedly tells Christians that they must put on their new selves and live out their new lives. It is all too easy for us to slip back into old habits. We have to learn new patterns of thinking, new ways of treating other people and new habits that reflect our new selves: '. . . you have taken off your old self with its practices and have put on the new self, which is being renewed in knowledge in the image of its Creator' (Colossians 3:9–10).

The old self has gone, it's been taken off like an old coat, yet we still need to be actively ensuring we're not falling back into its practices. But wonderfully, we have put on Christ, who is our life. As we live in him, the new self we have put on like a fresh shirt is constantly being renewed, so that we need never fear we have spoiled it with our ongoing sinful habits. Christ has broken the link between sin and death by paying the full penalty for all our sins, future as well as past. Our ongoing sin no longer brings us death. This is the new 'law of the Spirit' that Paul describes in Romans 8:1–2, which brings us life.

The instructions given to Adam and Eve about how to live as humans were extremely limited. Their purpose was to fill the earth and rule over it; Adam was instructed to tend the garden and both were not to eat from the tree of knowledge. We no longer have access to the garden or the tree, but we may continue to fulfil our creation purpose with regard to filling and stewarding the earth.

Since the arrival of sin, God's instructions have needed to be far more specific and detailed. Since sin affects every part of us, including our ability to know what is right and good, we need God to tell us what we should do and how we should live. In our old humanity, even our best efforts to follow God's commands were doomed to failure. The law was a good thing, showing us what we should do, and making our inadequacy obvious to us. But the law could not change our lives.

The Spirit is not like the law! The Spirit also shows us how we should live, but the Spirit empowers us to live that way. Here's how Paul explains it in Romans 8:

> Those who live according to the flesh have their minds set on what the flesh desires; but those who live in accordance with the Spirit have their minds set on what the Spirit desires. The mind governed by the flesh is death, but the mind governed by the Spirit is life and peace. The mind governed by the flesh is hostile to God; it does not submit to God's law, nor can it do so.
> (Romans 8:5–7)

In the old humanity, we were governed by the 'flesh'. This is how Paul talks about our sinful nature. In this life, our minds were governed by our sinful nature. Sin determined what we wanted, how we thought, what we did. In this life, we did not obey God and we could not obey God. But in the new humanity, we are governed by the Spirit. It is the Holy Spirit that governs our minds now. The direction of our desires changes, so that we want to do what the Spirit wants. The Spirit affects our desires, our thinking and our doing. The Spirit enables us to follow God's law, so we should. Since we live by the Spirit, we should live according to the Spirit (Galatians 5:25).

The Holy Spirit lives and works in us, combating the power of our sinful nature, but we are still human beings, complete with both body and soul. The new humanity is still humanity; that is to say, all of the things Genesis 1 and 2 teach us about being human are still true: we are created in the image of God, we are male and female, we are body and soul, we are made to work and we are made for relationship. We do not become less human by being joined with Christ in this new humanity: we become more human. We don't become humanoid robots, our human body taken over, leaving us with no control. We still have our own mind, our own desires, our own inner being. The Spirit enables us to live our new lives, but he does not compel us to do so against our will. The Spirit teaches us to want what is good and right, but he does not override our wishes.

Our new life is characterised by an ongoing struggle between our old nature and our new nature, between sin and the Spirit. Sometimes the Spirit will kill one particular sin stone dead, perhaps at the moment we turn to Christ, or at some later time. When I became a Christian in my teenage years, I found that I immediately stopped blaspheming. I did not plan to do so, or have to work at it, learning new habits of speech. I just stopped overnight and have never been tempted to start again. If you have had a similar experience with a habitual sin that suddenly disappeared, praise God!

It is much more usual, however, to have to keep putting our sins to death. If you write a spiritual journal, I hope you take great encouragement from looking back to see how much God has changed you over the years. But I suspect there will be some prayers concerning ongoing sin that you have been praying for years and years. Perhaps you experienced relief from a particular sin for a time, only to have it return with a vengeance. Perhaps you were grateful not to struggle with certain kinds of temptation, until that moment when you did.

Our sinful nature is more deeply embedded than most of us realise. As we grow in the Spirit, it is normal to discover greater depths to our depravity than we ever could have guessed. That's one reason why older Christians are so often characterised by great humility – they are so much more conscious of their sin than those who are newer to the faith.

Humility is just one of the characteristics of new life in the Spirit. The Spirit produces fruit of love, joy, peace, patience, kindness, goodness, faithfulness, gentleness and self-control in us (Galatians 5:22–3). Our new self is compassionate and forgiving (Ephesians 4:32), and above all loving (Colossians 3:12–14). In this new humanity, we bear with one another, serve one another, honour one another, encourage one another and submit to one another. Where necessary, we admonish one another in order to help one another keep walking in accordance with our new life in the Spirit.

New life with a new purpose

This new humanity has a new purpose to add to the old one. We are given the task of filling the earth, not just with more people, but with more disciples:

> Then Jesus came to them and said, 'All authority in heaven and on earth has been given to me. Therefore go and make disciples of all nations, baptising them in the name of the Father and of the Son and of the Holy Spirit, and teaching them to obey everything I have commanded you. And surely I am with you always, to the very end of the age.'
> (Matthew 28:17–20)

Adam and Eve were to build the first humanity from their physical descendants. Christ is building the new humanity through the witness of his disciples. Our new lives are the evidence of this new humanity, as people see the Spirit at work in us, making us more holy, more like Christ. Our changed lives are the evidence that the gospel message we proclaim is true and powerful.

You and I are not capable of bringing new life to another person. We cannot do the work of the Holy Spirit in putting flesh on the dry bones and breathing God's Spirit into them. But when Jesus told the first disciples to go and make more disciples, from every nation, he assured them he would be with them always. How is Christ with them – and with us? By his Holy Spirit, of course.

That is the mystery of evangelism: as we obey Christ's command to proclaim the gospel and live accordingly, so the

Spirit works to bring people to new life. This is the purpose of the Church: to tell people the good news about Christ and to live in a manner worthy of it. As we do so, we can trust that God will be doing his work of saving souls.

We honour God with our new lives, both by living in obedience to the Spirit and by speaking the truth about Christ.

Questions to consider

1 If Christ has dealt with our sin, why do Christians continue to sin?
2 How does the Spirit transform us in our new lives?
3 What is your experience of putting sins to death in your own life? Can you testify to the power of the Spirit helping you with this? Are you in step with the Spirit in this work?
4 How are you involved in the task of proclaiming the good news of Christ? Is there something else you could do in obedience to this command?

13

Being adopted

The Spirit you received does not make you slaves, so that you live in fear again; rather, the Spirit you received brought about your adoption to sonship.
(Romans 8:15)

Some years ago, I was part of a new church plant that included a family who were in the process of adopting a little girl. She was one of those babies who made friends instantly, with her wide grin and confident curiosity about everything and everyone. Our church family loved her and welcomed her with open arms. As we supported the family through the process, and later as we all got to know Naomi, her adoption was a wonderful reminder for us all that we too had been adopted by God into his family.

Sometimes people think of adopted children as not quite the same as biological children. There are certainly examples of adopted children not being treated fairly, or having their lack of blood relationship used against them. But that was not how Naomi's adoption worked, and it is not how adoption is supposed to work. It is not how adoption worked in the ancient world, where adopted children had exactly the same status and rights as any biological children.

In modern Japan, adoption of adults is a common phenomenon. Families without male heirs choose to adopt men to take on the family business. Sometimes these are sons-in-law, but sometimes they are work colleagues. These adoptions are for the purposes of inheritance.

Our adoption into God's family is for the purposes of inheritance, but it is far more than that. As God's adopted children we are given all the rights and status of biological children. We are adopted into God's family because, through faith, we are united to Christ, the eternal Son. That's why older hymns and prayers refer to us all as God's sons, and indeed why many Bible translations continue to talk about adoption to sonship, even when they use gender-neutral terms elsewhere: because all of us, male and female, are adopted through the Son. We all, male and female, share in the same status, the same rights and the same inheritance in Christ, because we are all adopted as children of God. 'See what great love the Father has lavished on us, that we should be called children of God! And that is what we are! The reason the world does not know us is that it did not know him' (1 John 3:1). God's adoption of us is not merely to guarantee our legal status as his heirs. It is a lavish act of great love, which makes us into his dear children. As his children we are intimately known, deeply loved and graciously disciplined.

Intimately known

God has known each one of us intimately from the moment of our creation, and even before that. As the psalm says, before God created us in our mother's womb, he knew us (Psalm 139:13). But one of the effects of sin is to make us hide from God, just as Adam and Eve hid in the garden after they had sinned (Genesis 3:8). It's hard enough to have to confront the reality of our own deep sinfulness, let alone have anyone else see it and know what we truly are.

I remember talking to a friend many years ago after she had been married for a little while. She told me that she had never been so conscious of her own sinfulness as in those first months of marriage. The closer we allow someone to come to us and the more we reveal of ourselves to them the more our sin will be on display to us as well as to them. That kind of vulnerability is terrifying.

How much more terrifying when the person we are opening up to is perfectly holy. God has no hidden secret depths of sin to make us feel better when we share ours. The confession is all one-sided.

And yet there should be no fear, because 'perfect love drives out fear' (1 John 4:18). We are intimately known, but we are perfectly loved. We need not run and hide from our Father God. We can be completely honest with him, because he already knows all the darkest parts of our soul, and yet he has chosen us to be his children.

There is such security to be had in being fully known. We do not have to worry about being found out by God. We don't have to try to keep secrets from him and hope that we will get away with it. We aren't trying to put a good face on things while constantly sweeping our failures under the carpet.

Every single day, we can come to God and talk to him honestly about everything. Everything we've done and said and thought. Every desire we've had and every temptation we've felt. Every time we've been over-confident about our ability to resist temptation and every time we've failed. Every shameful aspect of our character. Every moment of selfishness or pride. We can admit it all to him, certain that he already knows us and still loves us.

He knows our sin, but he also knows our needs. The God who made you and knows you in your deepest being understands you completely. He understands all the ways in which you are different from other people. He knows that you need friends and family, but also that maybe you need time alone. He knows that you need purposeful work, but also that you need time to rest properly from that work. He knows the joy you will find in your grandchildren, or the delight you have in enjoying creation, or the happiness that comes from using your musical talents.

> And do not set your heart on what you will eat or drink; do not worry about it. For the pagan world runs after all such things, and your Father knows that you need them. But seek his kingdom, and these things will be given to you as well.
> (Luke 12:29–31)

God knows what we need and he will provide for those needs. God delights to answer the prayers of his children in the way that gives them what is best for them (Luke 11:11–13). Sometimes even the people who love us most and know us best will give us presents that miss the mark. We open the wrapping paper and wonder what on earth they were thinking. I have no poker face at all, and I am not good at hiding my confusion and disappointment in those moments, which makes things awkward for everyone. When God gives us gifts, he always gets it right. Even if we are slow to understand what he is doing and why, we can trust that he knows what we most need, and what will be the best thing for us, because he knows us, more deeply and intimately even than we know ourselves.

Deeply loved

The reason we can be intimately known without fear is that we are also deeply loved. We can be absolutely sure of this, because God has demonstrated the depth of his love in the death of his most precious, beloved, eternal Son, Jesus Christ:

> This is how God showed his love among us: he sent his one and only Son into the world that we might live through him. This is love: not that we loved God, but that he loved us and sent his Son as an atoning sacrifice for our sins.
> (1 John 4:9–10)

God showed us just how deeply he loves us by sending his Son to live for us and to give us new life through him. He sent his Son to die for us, as a sacrifice for our sins, to make atonement for us, so that we could be made right before God.

Atonement, like redemption, involves payment. Not of a price but of a penalty. Our sin deserves punishment. We have done wrong and God's justice demands that wrongdoing should be punished. The entire legal system of the Old Testament was based on this principle: wrong actions should be punished accordingly. The law demanded 'an eye for an eye and a tooth for a tooth' so that punishment could not be escalated beyond what each crime merited. But every crime merited its appropriate punishment.

When perpetrators of horrific crimes are brought before the courts, they can sometimes earn multiple life sentences. They do not have multiple lives to pay those sentences, and the point of the judgement is to make it clear that their penalty will never be fulfilled. They will never have been punished enough for what they have done. Their situation is hopeless.

If we were to stand before God, with every sinful act and word and thought and desire from our lives itemised, and the appropriate punishment calculated and tallied, we too would receive multiple life sentences. In our sinful nature, everything we do is directed away from God and away from what is good. Everything deserves God's just punishment.

But God loves us anyway. Even while we were his enemies, Paul says (Romans 5:10), God sent his Son so that we could be reconciled to him. Even while we were sinners, turned away from him, deserving only his punishment, God loved us.

And so, God paid the punishment we justly deserved. God, in the person of Jesus Christ, took our sin and sacrificed himself. He paid all our life sentences with his one infinitely valuable life, given over to death. He made the atonement that we never could. Because he loves us.

Parents will do extraordinary things to protect and save their children. They will shield their children with their own bodies, putting themselves between their child and a speeding car – or a speeding bullet. Parents struggling to put food on the table will make sure their children have enough, even if it means they go without. Parents who love their children sacrifice their own needs and even sometimes their own lives, if they have to. That is what love demands.

That is what the Father's love is. He loves us so much he was willing to sacrifice his most precious Son. That is what the

Son's love is. He was willing to sacrifice himself for our sake. That is how loved you are in Christ. His death is the objective proof of God's love for you. If ever you are tempted to doubt you are loved, you can remember that Christ died and know just how deep his love for you goes.

If God loved us like that when we were his enemies, enslaved to our sinful nature and deserving only his punishment, how much more confident we can be of his ongoing love now that we are being renewed by his Spirit and brought into his family and turning towards him in faith. He loves us as our Father, and he delights in us as his children.

As human beings we were made in God's image, to love and to be loved. In Christ, we experience the deepest expression of that, because we are loved by God himself.

Graciously disciplined

Part of a parent's job is to teach their children how to live. This involves positive instructions, modelling good examples, and sometimes discipline for disobedience. Our heavenly Father uses all of these methods for teaching us how to live as his children.

He teaches us through his word, the Bible. Old and New Testaments are full of instructions for us on how to live as God's beloved people. God does not leave us in the dark wondering how he wants us to behave! He teaches us, and he also gives us teachers who can help us to understand his word better and apply it to our individual lives more consistently. His instructions are simple enough to be summarised in two commands: to love God and to love other people. But they are thorough enough to apply to every situation we find ourselves in throughout our whole lives. Scripture is sufficient for all our needs. We can always turn to God's word for the wisdom we need to help us make godly choices through the power of God's Spirit.

Of course, God has also given us the perfect example of how to live our best lives, in the person of Jesus Christ. While his life did not include every specific circumstance we may face, nonetheless he embodied every godly characteristic that we need to follow his example in our own situation. He shows us how to be patient, loving and kind. He demonstrates justice, goodness and faithfulness. Christ's self-control and his self-giving love teach us how to do the same.

Even with all God's good instruction and the wonderful example of Christ to follow, however, we continue to go wrong. We habitually follow the desires of our sinful nature and fall into the ways of our old lives. We are stupid and forgetful, slow to learn. We are stubborn and hard-hearted, and think we know better. We need the gracious loving discipline of our Father to correct us and teach us: 'Endure hardship as discipline; God is treating you as his children. For what children are not disciplined by their father?' (Hebrews 12:7).

The writer to the Hebrews knows that the Christian life is not always easy. As well as the normal suffering that comes from living in a broken world, Christians are also likely to face opposition and even persecution because of their faith. We will have to make hard choices that set us apart from our friends and families. We are called to sacrifice our own sinful desires in favour of doing God's will. And even though we know that all of this will be better for us in the end, it is still hard to go through.

So, the writer tells his readers to reframe their thinking. The hardship they are experiencing is to be endured as discipline. It has a purpose: to make them holy, to bring a harvest of righteousness and peace (Hebrews 12:10–11).

Plenty of times in our lives we voluntarily go through hard experiences in order to get a reward that makes it worthwhile. Women go through the pains of labour in order to enjoy the delights of having a child. Athletes endure gruelling training regimes in order to enjoy the satisfaction of winning. Students work through tedious lectures and exams in order to enjoy a career that they find fulfilling.

So it is for us as Christians. We must endure God's discipline of us through hardships of various kinds in order to enjoy the promised life of righteousness and peace. Peter describes this same process as being 'refined by fire' (1 Peter 1:6–7). The fiery trials and tribulations of this life will purify our faith, burning out the impurities of our sinful nature. It sounds painful and it often is. But it is worth it.

God does not punish us for his pleasure, like a sadistic schoolteacher. He does not punish us on a whim, to keep us on edge. God disciplines us as a loving father, so that we learn how to live better lives:

My son, do not make light of the Lord's discipline,
    and do not lose heart when he rebukes you,
because the Lord disciplines the one he loves,
    and he chastens everyone he accepts as his son.
(Hebrews 12:5–6)

Questions to consider

1 How does God show his fatherly love for his children?
2 God knows us intimately and yet loves us deeply. Why do we need to remember both these things together?
3 What means does our heavenly Father use to teach us how to live as his children?
4 Many people have bad experiences of human fathers. How does God redefine for us what a true father should be like? What advice would you give to a new father, based on this chapter?

14

Being a new humanity

For he himself is our peace, who has made the two groups one and has destroyed the barrier, the dividing wall of hostility, by setting aside in his flesh the law with its commands and regulations. His purpose was to create in himself one new humanity out of the two, thus making peace, and in one body to reconcile both of them to God through the cross, by which he put to death their hostility.
(Ephesians 2:14–16)

Through his death on the cross, Christ has created one new humanity, thus making peace.

Ever since sin came into the world, it has divided people. It set Adam against Eve in the garden. It caused Cain to murder his brother Abel, after which he had to go to another land and establish a separate people. Sin caused the people at Babel to build a tower in an attempt to reach God, after which people were separated by language, not merely distance. The sin of Sarah led to the birth and banishment of Ishmael, establishing a new nation. The sin of Esau led to the establishment of the Edomite people, Israel's enemies throughout the Old Testament. Sin separates friends and families, as well as tribes and nations.

Because we are sinners, we live in a world full of prejudice and discrimination, of hatred and enmity. People are divided by the colour of their skin or their ethnicity, by their class and their wealth. People are discriminated against because of their sex or their accent or the colour of their hair. All the glorious diversity of humanity that God created becomes, in our broken world, a source of conflict and division.

In the Bible, this is seen most deeply in the division between the Jewish people and the Gentiles. The Israelites, descendants of Abraham, were chosen by God as his treasured possession, not because of anything special about them, but simply because God set his love on them (Deuteronomy 7:7). The Israelites were not superior in themselves, but because of the privilege they had of being called the people of God.

Their role, in fact, was to serve the world and to bless the world. They were supposed to have made God known to the rest of the world, so that people from all nations would come to put their trust in him and be saved. By the time of the New Testament, however, the relationship between Jew and Gentile was not characterised by service or blessing. There was sharp enmity, as we can see from the Gospel narratives. Prejudice existed on both sides. Jewish people despised their fellow Jews who collaborated with the Roman – Gentile – occupiers of Judea. This deeply held divide continued into the early Church, where fierce debates about the status of Gentile Christians were finally resolved at the Council of Jerusalem in Acts 15.

Paul, the Jew above all Jews, with his exemplary lineage, education and zeal, is the apostle who most clearly understood what Christ has done to heal the divide. He argues strongly and persuasively that Jews and Gentiles are saved in Christ in exactly the same way. Gentiles do not need to become Jews – to be circumcised – in order to become Christians. In Christ, the difference between Jew and Gentile is erased. He created one new humanity. He made peace.

Living as one humanity

So in Christ Jesus you are all children of God through faith, for all of you who were baptised into Christ have clothed yourselves with Christ. There is neither Jew nor Gentile, neither slave nor free, nor is there male and female, for you are all one in Christ Jesus. If you belong to Christ, then you are Abraham's seed, and heirs according to the promise.
(Galatians 3:26–9)

If I had to pick a candidate for most misunderstood Bible verse, I think I might pick Galatians 3:28. It is a favourite verse for many people wanting to impose their own ideology on the Bible especially, at the moment, feminist ideology or even transgender ideology.

But Paul is not stupid. He is not suggesting that these categories no longer exist at all. In other places, he gives specific instructions to slaves and to free people, to men and to women. He understands that Jewish Christians remain Jewish and that Gentile Christians remain Gentile – this is the whole point of his argument in Galatians!

The context of Galatians 3:28 is specifically about salvation. In Christ, we have all become children of God, because we are all clothed with Christ. In Christ, we are all counted as descendants of Abraham, and heirs of the covenant promises made to him. The point is that there is no difference in the way we are saved, or in our status as saved people. Jews are not saved in a different way from Gentiles. Women do not relate to God in a secondary way, through their menfolk, but directly as children and heirs. Slaves and free men have completely different status in the world, but in Christ they become equals.

Gentiles do not need to become Jews to be saved. Women do not need to become like men in order to be saved. Slaves do not need to be freed by their masters, because they have become free in Christ. Whatever our earthly circumstances, in Christ we are all the same. We are all one in Christ Jesus.

That oneness is a beautiful thing. It should be one of the most powerful ways in which the Church can witness to the world. When Christians come together as one, across all the divisions that scar society, we bear witness to the saving work of Christ in reconciling people to God and thus to one another. Sadly, our churches can be infected by prejudice and division as easily as any other group of people.

Living together as one new humanity does not come naturally to us. The New Testament is full of instruction as to how we can do it. Two metaphors help us to understand what we are striving for: the building and the body.

Peter uses the image of the building in 1 Peter 2, where he calls us living stones being built together into a spiritual house, with Christ as our cornerstone. Again, it is Christ who is the source of our unity, holding the whole building together. Each stone has its place in the wall, resting on some stones and supporting others. A heap of bricks is neither useful nor beautiful, but when those bricks are carefully laid together on a strong foundation, they become much more than the sum of their parts. On our own, we can't be much of a building. Together, built on the solid foundation that is Christ, we become the Church, the people of God. Just as the whole building is stronger with each stone in its proper place, so the whole Church is stronger with each person there, supporting and being supported, holding each other up.

In 1 Corinthians 12, Paul uses the metaphor of the body to describe the Church. Bodies are made up of lots of different parts: eyes, ears, arms, hands and so on. The parts all need one another, and they all do different things. But they are united, they are one body, with a common goal and purpose. We have one head of this body, directing all the parts; that is, Christ. We are his body in the Church, united with one another because we are united with him. This metaphor is helpful for reminding us that unity is not the same thing as uniformity. We shouldn't expect or want the Church to be full of people who are the same as one another, any more than we would want a body entirely made up of ears. In this new humanity, difference and diversity are to be celebrated. We should be thankful for the people in our churches who are completely different from us – thanking God for their gifts and experiences, for their culture and their insight, and learning how to be a body working together in all our different parts.

How do we do that? We need to:

- honour one another (Romans 12:10);
- accept one another (Romans 15:7);
- carry one another's burdens (Galatians 6:2);
- be kind and compassionate to one another (Ephesians 4:32);
- forgive one another (Ephesians 4:32);
- submit to one another (Ephesians 5:21);
- look to one another's interests (Philippians 2:4);
- bear with one another (Colossians 3:13);

- love one another (1 Thessalonians 4:9);
- encourage one another (1 Thessalonians 5:11);
- spur one another on to love and good deeds (Hebrews 10:24);
- confess our sins to one another (James 5:16);
- pray for one another (James 5:16);
- offer hospitality to one another (1 Peter 4:9);
- and, above all, repeated again and again and again, love one another. Love one another. Love one another.

All the rest can be summed up in that one instruction: love one another. It is not a surprising instruction. It is the second of Jesus' two commandments summarising the whole of the law: love God and love your neighbour as you love yourself. It is supposed to be as natural to love other people as it is to love ourselves, but it is also true that many people struggle to accept that they are worthy of love themselves. I don't think Jesus is commanding us to spend years in therapy in order to learn to love ourselves before we can look to the needs of others, but I do think that Christians, as beloved, redeemed children of God, need to learn to view themselves in the right way. We are all precious human beings, made by God, loved by God, bought at a great price. God's love for us enables us to love other people freely and generously without putting ourselves down. God's love for others reminds us that we don't need to become their saviour, so that they depend on us rather than him.

Love is not to be restricted to our fellow believers. Christ also commanded us to love our enemies and pray for those who persecute us (Matthew 5:44). But love should be the overwhelming characteristic of the one new humanity created by Christ.

He has brought peace and reconciliation so that we may love one another. He has united us in his own body by shedding his own blood. How then can we fail to love those whom he has loved so deeply? How can we think of ourselves as better than them, when we know how desperately we were lost without Christ? How can we hold petty grudges, when he has forgiven so much more? In Christ we have received so much. Surely we will want to share it, freely and generously, with others.

It is hard. Of course it is hard. We are still sinners by nature and habit. We are still more conscious of the annoying cough of the woman who insists on sitting next us to in church than we are of her precious beloved status as a sister in Christ. We still value people according to the world's criteria: by their influence, their talents or their wealth, rather than by the Lord's criteria of humility, patience, love and faith. We judge people by how well they bear with us, love us, forgive us and show kindness to us, rather than by looking to ourselves to increase our own love, patience, forgiveness and kindness.

We need one another to spur us on in this love. We need to learn together how to be this new humanity, one in Christ, united in our faith, and loving one another.

The future of the new humanity

We are still learning. All local churches and all Christian people are still learning how to live as part of this new humanity. We all have blind spots as a result of our own upbringing and experiences, and as a result of the wider culture we come from. By their very nature, blind spots are almost impossible for us to notice. If we are used to living in a sexist culture, we will not find it easy to recognise our own sexism. If the world around us is deeply racist, our own racism is likely to go unexamined. We need a way of stepping back and seeing things differently.

That is what we get in the book of Revelation. As the curtain is lifted on the heavenly realm, we are shown an entirely different perspective on the world and the Church within it. Because the scene is so different from what we are used to on a Sunday morning, it should make us stop and reconsider. It gives us a new yardstick to measure up against and see where we are found wanting.

Here's how the Church is described in Revelation 5:

> . . . with your blood you purchased for God
> persons from every tribe and language and people
>   and nation.
> You have made them to be a kingdom and priests to
>   serve our God,
>   and they will reign on the earth.
> (Revelation 5:9–10)

Persons from every tribe, language and nation have been made into one kingdom. All of those voices, in all of those languages, join together in singing God's praise and serving him. Not in separate churches. They're not divided, with the Black church in one corner, the Asian church in another and the White church over there. They are one kingdom. One humanity.

That is what the Church should be like. It is what the Church is going to be like. It is what the Church needs to be like. But it is going to be hard work.

The Church as it is now, in the UK and in many other parts of the world, is too often divided by race. There are deeply painful historical reasons for this: slavery and colonialism. There continue to be appalling examples of institutional racism and personal racism – in the police force, in healthcare, in education. The Church is not exempt from this, but we should be the ones setting the example in finding ways to overcome it. We are one in Christ, so let us show it in our churches.

That will mean taking the actions listed in the previous section: confessing our sins, bearing with one another, praying for one another, being compassionate and kind to one another, forgiving one another. It will mean putting one another's needs before our own. It may mean being part of a church where things aren't what we are used to, where we are in a minority, where we don't feel valued and appreciated. It will mean being humble and patient. It will mean loving one another.

In the new humanity, it is not only racial divides that will be erased. Social divides based on class, wealth and sex will also be reconciled. When James and John bicker over who will have the seat of honour next to Christ, he tells them, 'Anyone who wants to be first must be the very last, and the servant of all' (Mark 9:35). In the topsy-turvy hierarchy of the kingdom, those qualities that make a person important in the world will be utterly unimportant.

No one in the Church should get pride of place because of their social status, as social status does not matter in the kingdom (James 2:1–4). It should be normal in all our churches for those who are wealthy to sit next to those who are struggling to make ends meet. It should be normal for those in high-powered jobs to be part of a church family with people who are on benefits. People of lower social status should be respected as leaders with authority over those of higher social status. Women should be valued as highly as men. Children should be welcomed and older people should be honoured.

We should never ever find ourselves suggesting that someone might be more comfortable at another church, where there are more 'people like them'. Whatever our external differences, we are all one in Christ. We are brothers and sisters in the household of God. And so, whatever it takes, we need to welcome our family in. We need to honour them and love them. We need to be thankful that we have another different part of the body. We should rejoice whenever our church family becomes a little bit more like the church we are going to become.

We should delight in the opportunity to express our one new humanity in Christ.

Questions to consider

1 What are some of the obvious differences that exist in your own church family? Do these differences lead to joyful diversity, or simmering disunity? In what ways could you better reflect the oneness of the new humanity we all share in Christ?

2 Read through the list of instructions given in this chapter for learning to live as one body. Can you think of specific examples where these are put into practice in your church?

3 Which of these do you think you need to do better at? Again, think of specific situations or particular relationships where you need to show more love.

4 How well does your church family reflect the diversity of your local community? Is there anything you could do to reach out to under-represented groups and welcome a more diverse group of people into your church?

15

Being raised to eternal life

Time always moves in the same direction. Things move forward and never backwards. Dirty plates can be washed clean again, but baked cakes can't be separated back into their ingredients. We can't unlive our past experiences, even if sometimes we can unpick the consequences of our actions.

There is no way back into the garden of Eden as it was before the fall. We cannot unlive the experience of sin and its consequences. The promise of the gospel is not that we will go back to the time of the first creation. The promise is that we will go forward to a far better future in the new creation.

In that new creation we will be more human than ever before. Just as the first Adam was created body and soul, so we will be raised body and soul. But where the first Adam became mortal, we will be raised immortal. The first Adam was placed in the heavens and earth to rule and subdue, and to work the garden. The second Adam was brought to new life in a garden, but will bring the new heavens and a new earth into being. When we are raised to new life in Christ, the entire creation will be renewed for us to inhabit. We will finally fulfil all that God created us for. His purposes for humanity will be complete in us.

Raised with immortal bodies

On the first Good Friday, the dead body of the Lord Jesus was laid in the tomb. On the third day, when the women went to perform the mourning rituals, the body had gone. His resurrection was not some kind of spiritual metaphor, but a physical reality: he broke bread, he ate fish, and Thomas touched his scars. At Christ's resurrection his physical body was reunited with his soul.

Jesus' resurrection is the first fruits, the forerunner, of the great resurrection. His resurrection body is the example of what ours will be. If his resurrection was bodily, we can be confident that ours will also be bodily. Christ's resurrection body was recognisably him – even if it did take disciples who weren't expecting to see him again a while to realise who they were walking and talking with. I think we can expect our resurrection bodies to be recognisably ours too. We won't be transformed into Hollywood film stars or catwalk models. Our beauty will be seen in the glorious diversity of humankind no longer worn down from the hardships of living in a broken world, or distorted by the consequences of our own or other people's sin. In Christ's resurrection, his scars were visible but not disfiguring. The wounds of the Lamb who was slain were glorified because of what they signified. Where we have scars that speak of our endurance through this life, those scars will be celebrated as marks of honour.

Our resurrection bodies will be healed: the blind will see, the lame will walk, the mute will shout for joy. If we have suffered in this life from disease or disability, we will be wonderfully renewed in a way that glorifies our Creator and Re-creator. We will not find ourselves frustrated by our physical limitations in the way that we currently are. Probably we will not all run with the speed of a Usain Bolt, but we will all have the capacity we need to live our lives to the full. The exhilaration of marathon runners, mountain climbers and sky divers will be within grasp for all of us.

Every physical delight will be ours in the resurrection. One of my favourite pictures of the resurrected life is found in Isaiah, where God promises a fine banquet for his people, full of rich meats and fine wines. It will be a meal far more delicious than anything served in a Michelin-starred restaurant, accompanied by wine far smoother than anything produced by Château Lafite. The wedding supper of the Lamb will eclipse every royal wedding banquet ever seen.

There is one respect in which our resurrection bodies will be different from our bodies now:

> So will it be with the resurrection of the dead. The body that is sown is perishable, it is raised imperishable; it is sown in dishonour, it is raised in glory; it is sown in weakness, it is raised in power; it is sown a natural body, it is raised a spiritual body.
> (1 Corinthians 15:42–4)

Our perishable, mortal bodies are like seeds sown in death. But as seeds grow into plants that are far more glorious than the original husks, so too our bodies will be raised into new bodies more glorious than the original.

Death, you remember, entered the world as a consequence of sin. It is not a necessary part of human nature but a broken part of sinful humanity. In the new creation, there will be no more death. There will be no sorrow, no sickness, no separation and no sin. There will be none of the struggles that make us sometimes long for an end to our suffering, even if that means an end to life. It is hard for us to imagine an endless existence of delight, without any fear or anxiety about the future.

This is not an infinity of idleness, of course. Work was a good part of God's good creation and, freed from all the frustrations brought about by God's curse on Adam, it will be a satisfying part of our resurrection life. Our purpose will be, as in this life, to honour God and obey him. We will be fulfilling the creation mandate to rule and subdue the creation. When we have beaten our swords into ploughshares and our spears into pruning hooks, we will be equipped for the work of tending the land. The new creation is described in Revelation 21 as a city rather than a garden, so it seems likely that there will be all kinds of work for us to do: temple work, sanctuary work, creative work, collaborative work. Work that God has prepared in advance for us to do, and work that God has prepared us to do.

Paul tells us that these imperishable bodies are raised in glory, in power and in spirit. Our lives now are full of dishonour and weakness, because of our sinful nature. In the resurrection we will be free of all these things. We will be free to live as the humans we were always designed to be.

This is the life we have to look forward to, but it is also the life we can look to now. We have been raised with Christ and our life is with him, not in this world. This is why Paul tells the Colossians:

Set your minds on things above, not on earthly things. For you died, and your life is now hidden with Christ in God. When Christ, who is your life, appears, then you also will appear with him in glory.
(Colossians 3:2–4)

We may not have the freedom of our resurrection bodies yet, but our lives are already hidden with Christ. His resurrection is the sure and certain guarantee of ours, because he is our life. Our thoughts and goals, our desires and our actions, must be set towards heaven, since that is our destination, our citizenship and our life. For now that is our hope, but one day it will be our reality. When Christ returns on the day of his glory, we too will appear with him in glory. Our bodies and souls will be reunited in him, and raised to glory in him.

Raised in a new creation

Life in the new creation, the new heavens and the new earth, will be different because our resurrection bodies will be different, and because our sinful nature will have been destroyed for ever. It will also be different because the creation itself will have been restored.

At the moment, the whole universe is affected by sin. The ground itself was cursed by God as a result of Adam's sin. Paul describes the creation as 'groaning' while it longs for its restoration (Romans 8:22), as if it were a woman in labour, groaning as she longs for the arrival of her child. The groaning of creation is seen in what we think of as 'natural' disasters: earthquakes, volcanic eruptions, hurricanes and tsunamis. The tendency of all things to decay and die is an indication of the groaning of creation: mighty oak trees are felled in a storm; stone cliffs erode with the constant washing of the sea; fields and gardens get choked by weeds without constant maintenance. We live in a world that tends towards destruction and it is an ongoing struggle to keep it at bay.

The desert and the parched land will be glad;
   the wilderness will rejoice and blossom.
Like the crocus, it will burst into bloom;
   it will rejoice greatly and shout for joy . . .

Water will gush forth in the wilderness
   and streams in the desert.
The burning sand will become a pool,
   the thirsty ground bubbling springs.
In the haunts where jackals once lay,
   grass and reeds and papyrus will grow.
(Isaiah 35:1–2, 6–7)

The new creation will be rejoicing, not groaning! The land itself will be shouting for joy as it bursts into bloom. The deserts will come to life with running water and all the plants that follow. In England, it can be hard to imagine just how dramatic this vision is. Even in our driest summers, there are still green plants to be seen. In the Middle East and North Africa, by contrast, floodplains will become barren deserts of dust in the dry seasons when the land is parched. But when the rains come and the rivers burst their banks, the land does indeed burst back into life. The seeds that have been lying dormant in the ground germinate quickly to make the most of the growing season. Almost overnight, dry earth becomes lush growth.

This is the picture Isaiah gives us of the new creation. Where this world is like dry earth, infertile and hard to work, the new creation will be fertile ground, lush with growth and free of danger. For in the wilderness, there are wild animals, jackals lying in wait to hunt. But in the renewed land, those haunts become places of fresh growth to harvest. Work, in this new creation, will be a satisfying endeavour, fruitful and productive. It will give us a purpose that can be fulfilled, the delight of doing the thing we were designed for and were intended to do. It will be a joy for us and give glory to our Creator.

It is not just the agricultural and horticultural aspects of creation that will be renewed, and the work given to us to do will not all be farming and gardening. The Bible shows us humanity's move from the garden of Eden into the city of Zion. To be sure, it is a city full of trees, with a river at its heart, reminding us of the first garden. But a city is a different kind of society from a garden. There is culture and structure and a different way of living in a city.

Often in the Bible, as in contemporary life, cities were dangerous places. City streets were dangerous for women, but so were city homes and city mobs. Cities were places where sin could develop in the most devious, twisted ways, gaining ground in the dark alleys and the hidden rooms.

The new city will not be like that. The new city will be flooded with light, so that the darkness of sin cannot find a foothold.

The city does not need the sun or the moon to shine on it, for the glory of God gives it light, and the Lamb is its lamp. The nations will walk by its light, and the kings of the earth will bring their splendour into it. On no day will its gates ever be shut, for there will be no night there. (Revelation 21:23–5)

There will be no night; that is to say, there will be no darkness, no secrets, no hidden places and no sin. The glory of God will be the light that exposes everything, and the Lamb will be our lamp. We will have nothing to fear, because everything will be seen and everything known. We will be safe in this city, so we'll be able to delight in being there, in the presence of God, enjoying his new creation, doing the work we were intended for. Presumably some will be cooking up the great feasts, while others will be pressing the grapes to lay up for our fine wines. Artists and architects will be working with gemstones and precious metals to embellish the glorious temple-city that sparkles with God's glorious light.

It is hard to imagine what an eternity of life will be like in the new heavens and new earth. It's hard to understand how it will be continually satisfying and interesting, and we won't grow bored. Those of us who sometimes tune out towards the end of a longer-than-usual church service may be wondering how we will manage to keep praising God for ever.

And yet it won't be boring or repetitive. We won't be grumbling and moaning, looking back to this life and wishing we could indulge ourselves in our old habits of sin and selfishness. We will, finally, be living our best lives. We will be the people we were made to be. And we will be with God.

Being cut off from God's presence is the thing that has spoiled our lives ever since Adam and Eve were banished from the garden. They were sent out from God's presence. The ground was cursed and their lives were cursed, and the serpent was constantly there to deceive and destroy them. But all of those were simply symptoms of the underlying problem: they were no longer able to live in the sanctuary, the safe place, God's dwelling place.

One important way to understand the Bible's account of human history is as God bringing his people back into his presence. Individuals such as Moses were invited to stand on holy ground, but the fearsome fire and thunder was a strong warning to anyone who dared come uninvited into the presence of God. The ark of the covenant travelled with the people, but when it was touched by Uzzah, he was immediately killed. The ark was kept in the holiest place in the tabernacle and the temple, a place that had multiple layers of protection, because anyone who entered without due precaution would likewise be killed. Throughout the Old Testament, God's presence with his people was extremely limited and heavily guarded.

The coming of Christ marked a new era: 'The Word became flesh and made his dwelling among us' (John 1:14). God, in the person of Christ, made his dwelling here on earth, among his people. Had you lived in Judea in the early part of the first century, you could have seen him, talked to him and even touched him. And you would not have died as a result.

Most Christians did not live in that place at that time, and we haven't had that face-to-face encounter with Christ, but we do have God's Spirit dwelling within us. There is no physical symbol of God's presence as there was in the holy of holies, but our own bodies have become God's temple (1 Corinthians 6:19). Through Christ's death, we now have access to the very throne room of God (Hebrews 10:19–20). We can indeed come into God's presence safely, because we are in Christ, and he has redeemed us from our sin.

There is, however, much more to come. Now we see dimly, but then we shall see him clearly, in all his glory.

Look! God's dwelling-place is now among the people, and he will dwell with them. They will be his people,

and God himself will be with them and be their God. 'He will wipe every tear from their eyes. There will be no more death' or mourning or crying or pain, for the old order of things has passed away.
(Revelation 21:3–4)

God will dwell with us. He will be with us and be our God. He will wipe every tear from our eyes. It is the most beautiful picture of the tender intimacy we will experience with God in the new creation. He will be present with us. Not as a terrifying, inaccessible tyrannical dictator. We will not fear overstepping the mark and being destroyed by his holiness. Rather, we will see him face to face. He will stand before us as a loving father, gently wiping away our tears and showing us that there is no more reason for sadness.

In the new creation there will be none of those things that bring sorrow into our lives. No death or mourning, no crying or pain. No sadness and no sickness. No separation and no anxiety. No fears for the future or guilt from the past.

Instead, we will have Christ. We will have the Father and we will have the Spirit. Their eternal, loving relationship will include us within it. And we will finally know what it means to be truly human.

Questions to consider
1 What will be better about resurrected humanity compared with our present lives?
2 What aspects of the humanity we experience now will continue in the new creation?
3 What will be different about the world we inhabit then and what difference will this make to our lives?

4 How does the Bible's description of our eternal future help us to understand more fully what it means to be human?
5 Think back over everything you've learned from this book about being human. Make a list of all the things you can thank God for in your humanity, and spend some time in prayer and praise to him.